HEINEMANN • ENGLISH • LANGUAGE

H·E·L·P

WITH

IDIOMS

JANE APPLEBEE
ANTON RUSH

HEINEMANN

Heinemann International
A division of Heinemann Publishers (Oxford) Ltd,
Halley Court, Jordan Hill, Oxford, OX2 8EJ

OXFORD LONDON EDINBURGH
MADRID PARIS ATHENS BOLOGNA
MELBOURNE SYDNEY AUCKLAND SINGAPORE TOKYO
IBADAN NAIROBI GABORONE HARARE
PORTSMOUTH (NH)

ISBN 0 435 28116 X

Illustrations by Jane Applebee and Satoshi Kambayashi
Designed by Helen Hible

Phototypeset by
Advanced Filmsetters (Glasgow) Ltd
Printed and bound in Great Britain by
The Bath Press, Avon, England

92 93 94 95 96 97 10 9 8 7 6 5 4 3 2 1

CONTENTS

Acknowledgements

Our thanks are due to the following for their kind permission to reproduce a text or illustration:

Jane Bidder, 'How to win on sports day', *The Times*, 19.6.91, p 105; *Cosmopolitan* (UK Edition), 'Junking Junk Mail', February 91, p 98; by permission of Duckworth, 'The Multi-Movement Tabby Silencer' from Absurdities by Heath Robinson, p 13; *Daily Mail*, 'Libel Judge says sorry for slandering his "clapped-out Volvo"', 10.6.89, p 98, 'If you want romance, get a good lawyer', 14.6.91, p 100; *Evening Standard*, 'Why I've lost faith in the Police', 4.10.91, p 111, 'Four days of drinks on the empty house', 9.10.91, p 112, 'It's still a man's world at the office', 19.9.91, p 111, 'Thames Television—Coronation Street', 9.10.91, p 112, 'We don't whinge, we're just unloved, say teachers', p 100; *The Guardian*, 'Chocolate soldier stands test of time', 17.6.91, p 100, 'NHS policy chief attacks shake-up "gobbledegook"', 13.6.91, p 104, 'Soundbites', 20.6.91, p 106; *Human Resources Magazine*, 'Headhunting without Headhunters', Summer 91, p 111; *In & Around the London Pavilion*, 'Rock Island Diner', February 91, p 100; *The Independent*, 'Lenin looks on as Moscow dabbles in stock market', 20.6.91, p 106, 'German MPs capitalise on gobbledegook', 20.6.91, p 110, 'Young love and ordinary murder' by Sandra Barwick, 7.12.91, p 112; *Mail on Sunday*, 'The face of a lost innocence', 28.4.91, p 98, 'How true love is hammered home', 10.6.89, p 99; *News of the World*, 'Ursula to wed toyboy', 13.8.89, p 99; John Colley, 'A Doctor Writes', *The Observer Magazine*, 4.8.91, p 110; *The Sun*, 'The Di and Arfur Show!', 20.6.91, p 106, 'Zealots have soured our Euro vision', 20.6.91, p 106; © Times Newspapers Ltd 1991, *The Sunday Times Magazine*, 'Homes from Home' by Paul Duncan, 7.7.91, p 110; *Time Out Magazine*, 'Blithe Spirit', 10.1.90, p 99; © Times Newspapers Ltd 1991, *The Times*, 'ITN's flagship sails on without Sir Alastair' by Melinda Wittstock, 19.11.91, p 105, 'Bush running America from hospital bed' by Martin Fletcher, 6.5.91, p 104; *Today*, 'It's raining cats not dogs', 20.6.91, p 105, 'How to master hype', 24.7.90, p 104; Barrie Tracey, 'The pop stars' idol who hit rock bottom', *Sunday Magazine*, *News of the World*, 24.8.91, pp 110, 111; P Walker, 'Gemini', *Evening Standard*, 25.5.89, p 99; *The Wandsworth Guardian*, 'Residents warn: "Footpath has become a mugger's paradise"', 13.6.91, p 104; Christopher Zinn, 'Outback Odyssey', *7 Days*, 4.6.89, p 105.

While every effort has been made to trace the owners of copyright material in this book, there have been cases where the publishers have been unable to locate them. We would be grateful to hear from anyone who is unacknowledged.

INTRODUCTION

English-speakers like using idioms and colloquialisms because they add 'spice' to the language. However, they are often areas of difficulty for students of English. Even if you have a good command of English and can make yourself clearly understood, how good is your knowledge and understanding of idiomatic phrases and expressions? For example, do you know what *gobbledegook* means?

gobbledegook (see page 46)

Help with Idioms helps you to enrich your language and understand native speakers more easily. Saying *She was angry with me* will communicate your meaning adequately, but to say *She tore me off a strip* is far more evocative and exciting.

Help with Idioms explains and practises a selection of idioms commonly used in everyday English. There are approximately 150 entries which are divided into seven sections for easy reference. Every section has its own introduction giving further details about the particular group. For example, the introduction for **Slang** explains what it is and when it is used.

Before using these idioms, it is important for you to fully understand their meaning. Idioms have very specific applications which are not obvious from simply knowing the individual words. Most of the words included can be safely used in all situations, but care must be taken if using them in a written context. Idioms which need particular care are marked with a warning sign ⚠.

The meaning and usage of each entry is clearly explained. Phrases which have a similar meaning are cross-referenced in the book and the differences are explained.

Each idiom is followed by an amusing dialogue showing how it is used in context. The origin of the idiom is given and pronunciation is included if useful. Many of the selected idioms have fascinating historical origins, some are modern inventions which have only been in use for a few years or even months, some have been 'borrowed' from other languages, some are slang. Much research has gone into finding the origins of the words but there is sometimes more than one theory when the expression is very old. You may know alternative theories not included here!

There is a wide variety of exercises to practise and check your knowledge of the expressions. Many of the texts are authentic clippings from newspapers and magazines, which gives some idea of how frequently idioms are used.

The entertaining illustrations will help you remember the idioms, but please note that most of the pictures show the literal meaning of the words, not the idiomatic meaning. In other words, they are not visual definitions and do not explain the meaning of the idiom.

We hope understanding and using these idioms will help you to sound less like a learner of English and more like a native speaker.

HISTORICAL IDIOMS

The expressions in this category have a historical origin. They were first used many years ago, sometimes even centuries ago, to describe familiar events or situations—for example, buying food at a market, cutting wood, or gambling. Some of them are associated with real people who were famous in their day, such as Thomas Hobson who owned a stable of horses, or John Dennis who was a playwright. Today, even though their meanings may have changed or developed, the expressions are still used. Most native English speakers, who use these words and phrases in everyday conversation, don't know the stories associated with them. They are often amazed to learn that a common expression like *pay through the nose* has a logical explanation.

bark up the wrong tree
be on cloud nine
be on tenterhooks
be up to scratch
blarney
blow hot and cold
blue stocking
buff
business as usual
buttonhole someone
carry the can
catch someone on the hop
chips are down (the)
cliffhanger
eat humble pie
give someone short shrift
give someone the cold shoulder
Heath Robinson

Hobson's choice
keep up with the Joneses
let the cat out of the bag
look a gift horse in the mouth
mind your Ps and Qs
money for old rope
one for the road
pay through the nose
run the gauntlet of something/
    someone
sour grapes
steal someone's thunder
stick one's neck out
toe the line
turn the tables on someone
underdog
upset the applecart
white elephant

bark up the wrong tree

verb

be mistaken/direct one's attention towards the wrong thing or person

> A: The police came to my house today and accused me of stealing a diamond necklace. They said it had been taken from Lady Badger's house at 1.00 am.
>
> B: And had you done it?
>
> A: No, they were *barking up the wrong tree* as usual. I was miles away robbing a bank in Manchester at 1.00 am!

This expression originates from racoon hunts in America during the 19th century. The racoon is a wild animal which is about the same size as a cat and its fur used to be highly prized. The hunters' dogs would chase a racoon up a tree and then lie at the bottom barking. When they found the dogs the hunters would know which tree the racoon was hiding in. However, if the dogs had made a mistake and there was no racoon in the tree, they were *barking up the wrong tree*.

bark up the wrong tree

be on cloud nine

verb

be very happy/elated

> A: I asked my wife to post off a coupon for the lottery so we could have a chance to win a million pounds. We've never done it before but I had a lucky feeling. I couldn't believe it when my wife told me we'd won.
>
> B: That's incredible! You must have *been on cloud nine*.
>
> A: Yes I was, until my wife remembered that she had forgotten to post the coupon. So we haven't won anything!

This expression originates from the US weather bureau which identifies different types of cloud. The highest type, which is found at over 10 000 metres, is called **cloud nine**. The association with happiness is through a play on words because **high** can also mean euphoric or elated.

be on cloud nine

be on tenterhooks

verb

wait anxiously for something

> A: I heard that you went to a haunted house and took photos of a ghost.
>
> B: Yes, I took them straight to the chemist and *was on tenterhooks* all week waiting for them to be developed.
>
> A: How exciting! So now you have proof that ghosts exist.
>
> B: No. Unfortunately the chemist threw them away. He said that every one had a strange white shape on it and so he thought I wouldn't want them.

This expression comes from the traditional method of cloth-making. Part of the process involved drying the cloth by stretching it over a wooden frame and securing it with hooks which were called **tenterhooks**. The cloth was stretched as much as possible so that it was under very great tension. The expression used today compares the tension of the cloth to the tension felt when one is very anxious.

See: CLIFFHANGER which describes a dramatic or anxious situation of which the outcome is uncertain.

be up to scratch
verb

be of an acceptable/desired standard

> A: I think you should go to the optician and find out if your eyesight *is up to scratch*.
>
> B: Why do you say that?
>
> A: Well last week I saw you talking to a lamp-post and asking it round for dinner!

Boxing was a common sport during the 18th and 19th centuries, but the rules were very different from those of today. The fight was not divided into bouts of a few minutes but continued non-stop until one of the men was knocked to the floor. Both fighters then had to go to a mark which had been scratched in the middle of the ring. If a man had been so badly injured that he could not **come up to scratch** within thirty seconds, he lost the fight and his opponent won.

The expression is often used in the negative—for example, *She wanted to be a singer but her voice wasn't up to scratch*. Other common forms are: *bring something up to scratch* and *come up to scratch*.

blarney
noun

persuasive/flattering/charming talk which is probably unreliable or untrue

> A: Did you hear about Mrs Readies, the rich widow? She met a wealthy businessman on holiday and married him.
>
> B: Is she happy?
>
> A: No, her husband was talking a lot of *blarney*. He isn't a businessman at all. He's an unemployed postman. It seems he only married Mrs Readies for her money!

The **Blarney Stone** is a rock set in the wall of Blarney Castle in Ireland. Tradition says that if you kiss the stone you will have the ability to charm and persuade people with your words. The tradition originates with McCarthy Mor who was the Lord of the castle. In 1602 he was attacked by English forces who demanded his surrender. Instead of admitting defeat immediately, McCarthy Mor kept giving the British excuses in order to delay his defeat. Because of his persuasive talking it took months before he surrendered.

blow hot and cold   *verb*

continually change one's mind about something/someone

> A: I can't understand it. First my wife says she wants to go to Paris with me and then she doesn't. Why do you think she's *blowing hot and cold*?
>
> B: Well it's a lovely romantic idea to take her there but perhaps she's worried that it will cost you a lot of money—hotels, air tickets, restaurants . . . you know.
>
> A: No, it can't be that. She'll be paying for everything!

This expression originates from one of the famous fables written by the ancient Greek author, Aesop. The story is about a man who meets a demon (small devil) in a wood. The man blows on his hands to warm them and so the demon invites him home and gives him a bowl of hot soup. When the man starts blowing on his soup to cool it the demon is terrified and throws him out of the house. The reason is that he is frightened of anything which can **blow hot and cold from the same mouth!**

blow hot and cold

blue stocking

a woman who is very intellectual or academic

> A: My brother's fiancée is definitely a *blue stocking*—quite honestly I'm surprised she wants to marry him. Sam left school at fourteen and has never read a book in his life!
>
> B: That's true, but on the other hand he does look like that tall, handsome actor, Tom Hunk!

Lady Elizabeth Montagu lived in London during the 18th century and held 'intellectual' parties at her home. Instead of gambling and gossiping, the guests listened to lectures given by learned people. A favourite speaker was the academic Benjamin Stillingfleet who talked about natural history and always wore blue stockings. As intellectual parties became popular, **blue stocking clubs** started all over London and their members wore blue stockings in admiration of Stillingfleet.

The reason that the expression is now only used to describe women may be because of the evolution of stockings. In the 18th century these were garments for both men and women. Today, stockings are only worn by women.

blue stocking

buff

a person who is devoted to a particular subject and therefore knows a lot about it/a knowledgeable enthusiast

> A: My son Fred goes to the cinema every night. He hasn't missed a day for three years.
>
> B: How interesting, I didn't know your son was a film *buff*.
>
> A: He doesn't know anything at all about films—he works in the box office selling tickets!

The word originated in the last century in New York City where amateur fire-fighters helped the official firemen to put out blazes. The amateur enthusiasts were called **buffs** because of their coats which were made out of **buff** leather. This was a pale yellow leather made from buffalo hide. Today its meaning has widened so that one can use it to describe people who are interested in many different subjects; you could meet *a wine buff, a music buff, a football buff* or *a chess buff* for example.

business as usual   *noun*

continuing as normal

> A: I've been a fortune-teller for thirty years so I was heartbroken when I lost my crystal ball. I went to see my friend Madame Jo-Jo who reads Tarot cards.
>
> B: Was she able to predict where you would find your crystal ball?
>
> A: No, but she did lend me her spare pack of Tarot cards—so now it's *business as usual*!

The wartime Prime Minister, Winston Churchill, is responsible for this expression. He first used it in a speech in 1940 during the Second World War, just after London had been bombed heavily. He said, 'The maxim of the British people is "**business as usual**"'—meaning that the population would carry on a normal life despite the bombs. Soon notices with the phrase appeared on buildings throughout the city—shops, offices, post offices and banks. Today it is not associated with war, but it is used to describe life continuing as normal despite problems or disasters.

buttonhole someone   *verb*

talk to someone who does not want to listen

> A: How was the party?
>
> B: Not very good. A dreadful young man *buttonholed me* and told me his life story. It took two hours!
>
> A: Never mind, it could have been worse. He could have been an old man and then it would have taken even longer!

This verb was originally to **buttonhold** and meant to hold on to the buttons of someone's coat. The idea was to sell goods to a reluctant customer by stopping him from walking away! Over the years the verb has become *buttonhole* and its meaning has grown to include talking to someone on any subject which the listener does not want to hear.

carry the can

verb

take responsibility or blame for something

> **A:** My friend Fred and I took my grandmother's old dog Shep for a walk in the park. Unfortunately, on the way home Shep was run over by a bus! Fred told me I would have to *carry the can* for the accident.
>
> **B:** Your grandmother must have been very angry with you.
>
> **A:** Well, I went to the petshop and bought a young dog which looked just like Shep. My grandmother couldn't tell the difference. She said that she'd never seen him so full of energy and asked me to take him out for walks more often!

This was originally a military expression. A group of soldiers would elect one man, usually of the lowest rank, to fetch beer for everyone. He would **carry** it in a large **can** (metal container) which he had to return at the end of the evening. So the man who *carried the can* took responsibility for it.

Now the phrase can be applied to anyone who has to take the responsibility or blame for something—rightly or wrongly.

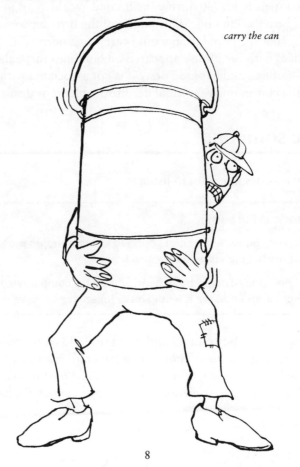

carry the can

catch someone on the hop

catch someone on the hop

verb

catch someone unprepared/surprise someone

> A: **Debbie had a baby a week after marrying Derek Dim. Derek didn't even know his wife was pregnant.**
>
> B: **Yes, the baby *caught him on the hop*—he thought Debbie was just very fat!**

The **hop** is a flower which is used in the brewing of beer and is traditionally grown in the county of Kent in south-east England. Just after the Second World War, hop-picking was a popular holiday for working-class Londoners as it was often the only chance they had to enjoy the countryside. It was a cheap family holiday which lasted the whole summer. Unfortunately, most men worked in jobs which gave only a few days holiday a year, and so they had to invent an excuse in order to go hop-picking. Sometimes the employer discovered the truth and **caught a man on the hop**, or in other words, caught him picking hops.

It is very common to use this expression in the passive. For example, *Make sure everything is ready well in advance otherwise you will be caught on the hop.*

9

the chips are down

a point during an important situation when you are forced to make a decision or take action

> A: I heard about a woman who survived a plane crash in the jungle and had to live for three weeks on worms and insects! I could never do that—I'd rather starve to death.
>
> B: I disagree. I think that if *the chips were down* you'd eat anything.
>
> A: Perhaps you're right. After all I do eat your cooking!

This expression originates from gambling. Bets are sometimes placed in the form of plastic counters called **chips**. When the chips are **down** or placed on the table the game is at a critical point because the players have committed their money.

cliffhanger

noun

a dramatic or frightening moment when one does not know what will happen next

> A: The captain announced the ship had hit something and was sinking. There was only one hour to get all the passengers and crew into the lifeboats. No one was sure if it could be done—it was a real *cliffhanger*.
>
> B: How terrifying. Who could have expected such a disaster?
>
> A: Well I must admit I was a little suspicious when I first boarded the ship and found it was called *The Titanic*!

The American actress Pearl White starred in a TV series called 'The Perils of Pauline'. Each episode would end with Pauline in a dangerous situation so that the audience would want to watch the next one to see what happened. In one episode Pauline was **hanging** on the edge of a **cliff** and this inspired the expression. *Cliffhangers* and *cliffhanger endings* are still used in TV drama series today. The expression can also describe situations in real life which are dramatic and uncertain.

See: BE ON TENTERHOOKS which means wait anxiously for something.

eat humble pie

verb

be very submissive after regretting an action or words

> A: Last week Charles accused his new secretary, Fiona, of stealing his wallet. It disappeared from his briefcase during lunchtime.
>
> B: How awful! I expect she lost her job immediately.
>
> A: No, Charles gave her a pay rise. The next day he found his wallet at home. It hadn't been stolen after all, so he had to *eat humble pie* all week and offer Fiona more money before she agreed to stay!

In the Middle Ages **umbles** were the unpleasant but edible parts of a deer which were cooked in a pie. The best deer meat was eaten by the rich, whereas the umble pie was eaten by their servants who were of a lower social class. Over time the word **umble** became confused with the word **humble** which means meek or submissive to give the current expression. It is often used in the following forms, *have to eat humble pie* and *make someone eat humble pie*.

See: KOWTOW which also means to behave humbly, but if you kowtow to someone, there is <u>not</u> a clearly defined reason for being submissive.

eat humble pie

11

give someone short shrift
verb

give someone very little of one's time due to impatience or annoyance

> A: When Mrs Tomlin takes her cat to the vet he spends ages with her, but when I go he *gives me short shrift*.
>
> B: Perhaps he likes Mrs Tomlin's cat better than yours.
>
> A: But I haven't got a cat, I've got a poisonous snake!

In the Middle Ages a prisoner who had been condemned to death was allowed a short time to confess to a priest before the execution. The Old English word for confession was **shrift** and so **short shrift** was the short confession that the prisoner made in order to receive forgiveness from God.

give someone the cold shoulder
verb

treat someone in a cold way/shun someone

> A: Don't bother to ask Mr Brown to help with the charity event—he always *gives everyone the cold shoulder*.
>
> B: Oh I'm sure he'll offer to help if I ask.
>
> A: Why is that?
>
> B: Because I'm his bank manager and he's overdrawn this month!

This expression is thought to come from a way of showing a guest he was not wanted! A welcome guest would be offered a delicious hot meal but an unwanted one would receive only cold food. **Shoulder** is a word for a cut of meat—for example, a shoulder of lamb—and so the phrase to *give someone the cold shoulder* literally meant to give someone cold meat—not a very appetising meal!

A derivation from this expression which has the same meaning is the shorter phrase *cold shoulder someone*.

strange-looking/appearing to be homemade or improvised (used about machinery/vehicles)

A: **Bob's father wouldn't buy him a VW for his birthday so Bob built himself a *Heath Robinson* car out of a bath, a motor bike engine and six bicycle wheels! He was really pleased with the result.**

B: **But surely it wasn't as good as a VW car.**

A: **No it wasn't, but Bob's father was so embarrassed every time his son drove around in it that he agreed to buy him a proper car!**

W Heath Robinson was a British artist who lived from 1872 to 1944. He became famous for his incredible cartoon drawings about inventors and their mad inventions. Today his name has entered the English language to describe any machinery or contraption which looks like part of one of his cartoons.

Heath Robinson (The Multi-Movement Cat Silencer)

Hobson's choice

noun

a situation in which there appears to be a choice when actually there is none at all

> A: Have you been to that chic new restaurant yet? I've seen the menu and there seems to be lots of delicious food.
>
> B: Take my advice—don't go. The menu looks very varied but it's always *Hobson's choice*. They never have anything available but fish and chips!

This expression was inspired by an Englishman called Thomas Hobson who lived in Cambridge during the early 17th century. He earned his living by working as a liveryman, hiring out horses to many of the university students. To make sure that every horse was used equally Hobson invented a special system. When a customer came to the stables, Hobson insisted that he chose the horse nearest the door. So although there were in theory many horses to choose from, in reality there was only one choice!

Common forms of the expression are: *It's Hobson's choice* (as in the example above) or *take Hobson's choice*.

keep up with the Joneses

verb

always buy/do what one's friends and neighbours buy/do in order to seem as rich as they are

> A: Marcia is always trying to *keep up with the Joneses*. When she found that all her friends had a car, she immediately bought one herself. It was such a silly thing to do.
>
> B: Personally I find a car very useful. Why do you think it was silly?
>
> A: Because Marcia can't drive.

Arthur R Momand, an American cartoonist, started writing a comic strip for the New York Globe in 1913 and it ran for 28 years. It was called 'Keeping Up With The Joneses' and came from his own experience of married life in Cedarhurst, Long Island where he had to buy things just to be equal to or **keep up** with his neighbours.

let the cat out of the bag
verb

reveal a secret by mistake

A: **I hid the money from the bank robbery in Gertie Gossip's house and told her to keep it a secret. But a week later she told her boyfriend by mistake.**

B: **I'm not surprised she *let the cat out of the bag*—she never thinks before she speaks. Don't worry I'll go and see her boyfriend and tell him to keep quiet. What's his name?**

A: **Detective Inspector Handcuff!**

Many country fairs used to sell piglets which were put in bags so that they could be carried home. Unfortunately some of the traders were not honest and put a cat, which was less valuable, into the bag instead of a piglet. It wasn't until the customer returned home that the *cat was let out of the bag* and the secret was revealed.

let the cat out of the bag

look a gift horse in the mouth

look a gift horse in the mouth   *verb*

be ungrateful for an unexpected opportunity/bonus

> A: **The Managing Director told me this afternoon that I could have a company car—a VW. But when I told him I would prefer a Ferrari he became very angry.**
>
> B: **I'm not surprised. After all you were *looking a gift horse in the mouth*! You probably won't get anything now.**
>
> A: **Yes I will. He told me I could have a bicycle.**

As a horse grows older, its gums recede and make its teeth look longer. So if someone looks inside a horse's mouth he is trying to check its age. The expression therefore described a situation in which someone found fault with a horse which was a gift. Nowadays the expression can be used in any situation in which somebody shows ingratitude for an unexpected present or opportunity.

If the phrase is used as a command, it always takes the negative form: *Don't look a gift horse in the mouth*.

mind your Ps and Qs   *verb*

be careful to be well behaved and polite

> A: **I'm going to have lunch with the Queen at the Palace.**
>
> B: **You'll have to *mind your Ps and Qs*. I've heard that she can be offended if visitors do or say the wrong thing.**
>
> A: **Don't worry. If I make a mistake, I'll offer to give her a ride on the back of my motorbike!**

This expression has two possible origins. It could relate to the old custom of recording the number of beers a customer had to drink. 'P' stands for pint and 'Q' for quart. A quart is two pints. English pubs do not use this measure now. Customers had the number and size of their drinks recorded by the barman using either **a 'P'** or **a 'Q'**. Before the customer left the pub he would be asked **to mind his Ps and Qs** or in other words, to pay his bill.

The second theory is that it was a warning to printers who used to put together metal blocks to make up a page of text. Each metal block had a letter on it which was backwards so that when printed it would appear the right way. Obviously, this meant it was very easy to mix up a 'p' with a 'q'.

money for old rope   *noun*

money for doing very little

> A: **Mrs Hallawell asked me to babysit for her last night. She said her baby, Francis, was very quiet and would sleep all the time. I thought it would be** *money for old rope* **but I'm never going to do that again.**
>
> B: **Babies can be very difficult to look after.**
>
> A: **No, he was fine but Mrs Hallawell's dog, Fang, didn't stop barking all night!**

In the Middle Ages hanging was a common death penalty. The hangman was the one who placed the noose around the neck of the condemned person and carried out the execution. He was paid for the job but could make extra money afterwards by cutting the rope into small pieces and selling them to the spectators. People used to think that the rope would bring them luck.

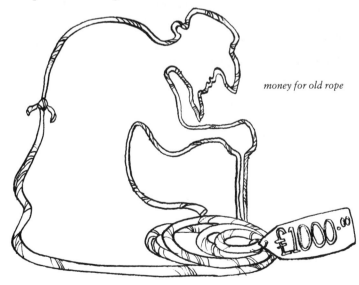

money for old rope

one for the road
noun

one last drink, usually alcoholic, before leaving a pub, house etc

> A: **It's a pity you have to leave the party so soon. If you're not in a hurry how about *one for the road*?**
>
> B: **Yes of course I can stay a little longer.**
>
> A: **Great. I've just invented a special cocktail. It's warm beer mixed with orange juice, whisky and strawberry jam!**
>
> B: **Err ... Actually I think I'll go now. I've just realised that I forgot to feed the cat. Goodbye!**

In London during the Middle Ages, prisoners who were condemned to death would be taken from the Old Bailey prison (now law courts) to Tyburn (now Marble Arch). The journey was along the straight road from the City to the West End in a wagon pulled by a horse. Before leaving, it was traditional for the prisoners to visit the pub opposite the Old Bailey. In the pub, the Magpie and Stump, they could have a large glass of beer or *one for the road*. The prisoners would arrive at Tyburn drunk and therefore would not worry about the execution to come!

pay through the nose
verb

pay a high price for something which is not worth it

> A: **It's my father's birthday next weekend, so I've invited him to London. I want to find him a really good hotel—the price doesn't matter. Do you know one?**
>
> B: **Well everyone says you *pay through the nose* at 'The Castle' but it is a lovely hotel. I would choose that if you're sure the price doesn't matter.**
>
> A: **That sounds perfect, I'm sure my father can afford it!**

This expression relates to a tax imposed by the Danes on the Irish during the 9th century. The punishment for not paying the tax was to have your nose slit open with a knife as an example to others.

See: RIP-OFF which is a slang term meaning cheat someone by making them *pay through the nose*.

run the gauntlet of something/someone   *verb*

suffer an attack/pressure/criticism

> A: **Did you hear about Freda Fib? Apparently she had to *run the gauntlet* of dozens of newspaper reporters when she arrived at a charity dinner in a real fur coat.**
>
> B: **But lots of people wear real fur, why did they decide to pick on Freda.**
>
> A: **Well, the dinner was in aid of the local animal rights group!**

Although gauntlet is an English word meaning glove, this expression has nothing to do with either England or gloves. It originates from the Swedish expression, **gatlopp** (**gata** means gate and **lopp** means course) which was a military punishment in the 17th century. Two lines of soldiers would stand facing each other and hit the punished man as he ran between them. Now *running the gauntlet* can refer to any situation which is unpleasant to bear because of the way you are treated.

sour grapes   *noun*

bitter comments about something which one wants but cannot have

> A: **That's a beautiful salmon you've caught. It must weigh over five kilos! Are you going to have it for dinner?**
>
> B: **Well I was, but when I showed it to Mr Surly he told me it was diseased and that it would be dangerous to eat.**
>
> A: **Don't listen to him—it's just *sour grapes*. He's fished in that river for years and he's never caught anything larger than an old boot!**

Aesop, the ancient Greek author wrote one of his many fables about a fox. The fox tries to reach a bunch of delicious grapes which is just out of his reach. After trying for many hours he eventually gives up. As he walks away he says to himself that the grapes are not worth having because they are probably sour. Of course the fox only has this opinion because he cannot have them— his opinion is just *sour grapes*. Remember that the expression is *never* used in the singular (sour grape).

sour grapes

steal someone's thunder

steal someone's thunder

verb

spoil the effect of someone's actions or words by doing the same or better first

> A: **In December I decided to wear a big hat with the words HAPPY CHRISTMAS on it. I thought that it would surprise everyone when I walked into the local bank.**
>
> B: **And did it?**
>
> A: **Not at all! I found that they'd *stolen my thunder*. The cashiers were in special fancy dress costumes—even the bank manager was dressed as a Charlie Chaplin! So no one even noticed me!**

This expression was first used by an English playwright called John Dennis who lived at the beginning of the 18th century. For one of his plays he invented a way to create the noise of thunder. Although the play itself was a disaster and soon closed, everyone loved the thunder sound effect! It was used by others so much that Dennis said, 'Damn them! They will not let my play run, but they steal my thunder'.

stick one's neck out   *verb*

do/say something which carries a high risk of failure, trouble or embarrassment

> **A:** **The Prime Minister** *stuck his neck out* **today and promised that the unemployment figures will be halved by the end of this year.**
>
> **B:** **That's good news—but what if he's wrong?**
>
> **A:** **He'll be unemployed!**

In the Middle Ages prisoners who were given the death sentence were often beheaded. The condemned person had to kneel down and place his neck or **stick his neck out** on a block of wood. The executioner then chopped off his head with an axe! Today the risk of *sticking your neck out* is not death but the result may still be unpleasant if you are wrong or fail!

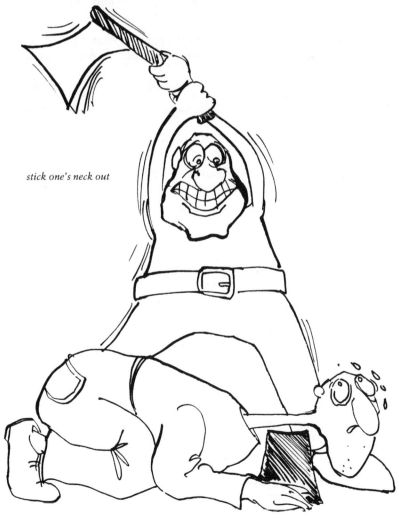

stick one's neck out

toe the line   *verb*

obey orders/accept the policy or ideas of a group

> **A:** My friends are going on a protest march in Trafalgar Square. They say it's very important and they expect me to come too. The problem is, I don't really want to.
>
> **B:** Don't worry. You don't have to *toe the line*. Just tell your friends you're going to do something else. What's the march about anyway?
>
> **A:** Human rights!

This expression comes from the House Of Commons, in the British Parliament, where two red lines are painted on the floor separating the members of the government from the opposition. A Member of Parliament who speaks is allowed to stand on the line but not to cross it. Originally the lines were set two sword lengths apart at a time when the MPs were allowed to take weapons into the room. If two MPs from opposing sides drew their swords they wouldn't be able to touch each other without crossing the line and breaking the rules of the House.

turn the tables on someone   *verb*

reverse the situation in which one is at a disadvantage so one is in a superior position

> **A:** When we were children we decided to have a competition and see who would become a millionaire first.
>
> **B:** George has always earned much more than you—it's obvious that he'll be the one to do it.
>
> **A:** Yes that's what I used to think but now I've *turned the tables on him*. Yesterday a solicitor rang me and said that a distant cousin has died, leaving me one million pounds!

This expression comes from the playing of board games such as chess and draughts. The games were originally played on special tables. If one player was losing and literally **turned the table** on his opponent then he would win the game.

It is often used in the passive—for example, *The tables were turned when I sent him the letter*. Remember that the expression is <u>never</u> used in the singular (turn the table).

See: TASTE OF ONE'S OWN MEDICINE which refers to the reversal of <u>unpleasant</u> situations.

underdog   *noun*

someone who is almost certain to fail/lose a competition/argument/war etc

> A: **Kevin Klumsy is the British entry at the Wimbledon Tennis Championships this year. He'll be the *underdog* as usual.**
>
> B: **Why do you say that? He might win!**
>
> A: **Well, for a start he's very shortsighted and has a wooden leg!**

An *underdog* can be a person, animal or country. A common way of using it is in the expression *support the underdog*. One theory about its origin is that it came from the time when dogfighting was popular. The dog who was strongest was called the **top dog** (which can be used of people today) and the animal who was more likely to lose was called the **under dog**. 'The Under Dog In The Fight' is a 19th-century song which ends:

But for me, I shall never pause to ask
Which dog may be in the right,
For my heart will beat, while it beats at all,
For the under dog in the fight.

underdog

upset the applecart

upset the applecart

verb

spoil a plan, arrangement or expected course of events

> A: **Did you go to Veronica Vain's wedding? I heard it was going to be the most spectacular social event of the year.**
>
> B: **Yes it was. On the morning of the wedding the groom *upset the applecart* by saying he couldn't go through with the marriage and wanted it all stopped.**
>
> A: **Oh no! What happened to the bride?**
>
> B: **Well, Veronica didn't want to disappoint the guests or waste the huge cake, so she married me instead!**

In the days when apples were taken to market in a cart along badly-made roads, it was easy for one of the cartwheels to become stuck in a hole. This would cause the cart to tip up or be **upset** unexpectedly and spill the apples on the ground. It is this image which is captured in the expression which is used today. Inanimate things as well as people can upset applecarts. For example, *The discovery upset the applecart.* or *His opinion upset the applecart.* It is also common to use an adjective to make the phrase more informative. For example, *upset the financial applecart* or *upset the domestic applecart.*

white elephant   *noun*

something which is expensive but useless/something which is costly to keep and has no apparent benefit

> A: I don't like my brother so when my uncle died and left him his MG sports car in his will, I was really pleased.
>
> B: That's funny! Weren't you jealous?
>
> A: No, not at all. You see the car is a complete *white elephant*; it uses an enormous amount of petrol and breaks down all the time. It's costing my brother a fortune.

This expression comes from Thailand where a long time ago there was a custom which the king would follow. Every time a **white elephant** was born in the country, the king would claim the rare animal immediately and keep it for himself. However if someone made the king angry or displeased him he would give the **white elephant** to that person. The reason was that the elephant was very expensive to look after and so would very quickly ruin the person who had annoyed the king.

white elephant

NEW IDIOMS

All languages change; words are forgotten or alter their meanings; new words are invented. During the last ten years there have been many inventions which have become popular enough to gain a place in the language. Many of these words have been spread through the media—television and newspapers in particular. This section will introduce you to a selection of commonly-used new words, some of which have become firmly established and are certain to still exist in ten years time.

bimbo	high-flyer
buzzword	hype
couch potato	junk food/junk mail
culture shock	moonlight
DIY	nightmare scenario
dosh	sell-by date
flagship	squatter
flavour of the month	state-of-the-art
freebie	thinking man/woman's (the)
ghetto blaster	toyboy
golden parachute	user-friendly
headhunt	yuppie

bimbo ⚠   *noun*

a young woman who is not very intelligent but is particularly attractive

> A: **Frank's new wife Marie looks exactly like the film star Marilyn Monroe. She's got blonde hair and always wears sexy clothes.**
>
> B: **She sounds like a *bimbo* to me. I thought Frank preferred intellectual women. What do they talk about?**
>
> A: **Marie is certainly not a *bimbo*—she's very brainy and works as a scientist. Most of the time they talk about nuclear physics!**

This word was originally used in America in the first part of this century. It was short for the Italian **bambino** meaning **baby**. However, it wasn't until the 1980s that the word became popular again and found its new meaning of **an attractive but stupid young woman**. A variation is **himbo** which can be used to describe a man with similar characteristics.

See: TOYBOY which describes a young man who is attractive.

buzzword   *noun*

a new word or expression which is fashionable

> A: **I've just started work in a record company and I can't understand a word anyone there says.**
>
> B: **Well there are so many *buzzwords* in the music industry, it takes time to learn them all.**
>
> A: **No that's not the problem. It's because they play music so loudly, I can't hear anyone speak!**

Examples of Sixties buzzwords are **cool** and **groovy** (very good, enjoyable); examples of Eighties buzzwords are **street cred** (in touch with fashion/ideas/opinions of the young people) and **power dressing** (dressing in clothes which indicate authority/ power) and examples of Nineties buzzwords are **green** (not harmful to the environment) and **ozone-friendly** (not harmful to the ozone-layer which protects the earth from the sun). Buzzwords often go out of fashion very quickly.

couch potato ⚠ *noun*

someone who is very inactive and spends most of their time watching television

> A: I went jogging eight weeks ago and broke my ankle. The doctor told me to stay at home and rest until it healed. All I could do was watch TV.
>
> B: How frustrating. When will you be able to jog again?
>
> A: Actually my ankle has already healed but I enjoy being a *couch potato* so much I've decided to give up jogging altogether!

This expression comes from America. **Couch** is another word for sofa or settee and **potato** refers to the idea that a person who just sits and watches TV becomes like a **vegetable**. **Vegetable** is a term for a person who cannot function as a normal human being, for instance, someone who cannot talk, move or think due to illness or injury.

couch potato

culture shock *noun*

feeling uncomfortable in a strange country or place because of the different habits and way of life

> A: Bobby is nine years old and has lived in London all his life. When his parents took him to the countryside for the first time it was a complete *culture shock*.
>
> B: What was he most surprised by?
>
> A: The cows. He'd thought that milk came from bottles!

This expression refers to any environment which is new and very different from one's own, and is therefore a **shock**.

household repairs or improvements which are done by oneself rather than by a professional or, able to be used easily without specialist skills or help from a professional

> **A:** We'd never done any *DIY* before, but when we moved into the dilapidated old house on the hill we decided to do the repair work ourselves. We thought that it would save money.
>
> **B:** That was a good idea. How much did you save?
>
> **A:** Well, by the time we'd bought all the tools we needed, such as saws, hammers, drills, chisels, screwdrivers and paintbrushes, we'd spent a fortune. So we didn't save anything at all!

This expression is an acronym standing for 'Do It Yourself' and was originally used by shops selling materials needed for home improvements and repairs such as putting up shelves or painting a wall, for example. The idea was that instead of paying a professional such as a plumber, builder or electrician you could **do it yourself** and save money. As a noun **DIY** can only refer to household improvements or repairs. For example, *My hobby is DIY*.

However, it can also, as an adjective, refer to other types of tasks or objects. For example, *I've bought a DIY dentistry kit to take on holiday with me* or *DIY heart tests are now available in shops*. In this second meaning, **DIY** refers to something which normally requires a professional or expert (dentist, doctor, lawyer, architect etc) but which has been changed to a form suitable for the amateur. It therefore cannot be used to describe everyday things like televisions, computers or cars.

See: USER-FRIENDLY which also can describe a machine which is simple to use.

dosh

noun

money

> **A:** Your husband looks very depressed at the moment. Is it money worries?
>
> **B:** Yes it is. I've just started my own company and I'm making far more *dosh* than he is!

Once a working-class word, **dosh** is now also used by young middle-class people. It generally refers to large amounts of money needed to buy such things as Porsches, houses and luxurious holidays. **Yuppies** and **high-flyers** often use it when talking about income. For example, *My new job pays £75 000 a year—that's a lot of dosh*.

flagship

something which represents the best that can be offered

> **A:** The 'beard tax' was the *flagship* of the last government. They said it was an important contribution to society. I agree with them.
>
> **B:** But nobody likes new taxes and a tax on men's beards seems very unfair. Why do you agree with them?
>
> **A:** Because it was so unpopular they lost the next election!

A **flagship** is the most important ship in a fleet. The expression can now be used to describe the most important or prestigous item of a series or group. For example, a radio programme, department store or publication can be a *flagship*.

flagship

flavour of the month   *noun*

currently popular/famous for a short while

> A: **Harry used to have no friends but now people phone him all the time to invite him to the pub.**
>
> B: **Why is he suddenly *flavour of the month*?**
>
> A: **Because he's started paying for everyone's drinks!**

This expression is thought to come from American ice-cream parlours which promote a different flavour every month. Another variation is **flavour of the week** which refers to something which is popular or famous for an even shorter time!

freebie   *noun*

something which is given free, often in return for possible favours in the future

> A: **I work as a journalist for a magazine about wine. The salary is quite low but there are lots of *freebies*. Most weeks I'm sent two or three bottles of wine by shops who want me to write articles about them. But there's one problem.**
>
> B: **What's that?**
>
> A: **I don't drink alcohol!**

This expression was originally associated only with journalists. As part of a promotion for a record, book, film or play, journalists are entertained with parties and given free samples and promotional material. Although there is no charge for these things the promoters will expect the journalists to repay them by providing free publicity in newspapers and magazines.

It can now be used more widely to refer to other situations in which something is given free with the hope of a response from the receiver. For example, if you buy a magazine and find a *freebie* inside (a sachet of shampoo perhaps) the manufacturer who has provided it hopes you will buy his product.

ghetto blaster

noun

a type of portable cassette player which can play music extremely loudly

> A: My grandmother loves music but she's getting deaf and couldn't hear her record player very well. She's solved the problem now.
>
> B: What did she do—buy a hearing aid?
>
> A: No. A *ghetto blaster*.

This expression came from America and became popular during the 1980s. **Ghetto** means a poor, urban area and **blast** means an explosion—in this case of noisy music. They are popular with young men, who carry them around in city streets (often in deprived areas). The volume is designed to impress other people rather than to entertain!

golden parachute   *noun*

a contract which is given to important executives so that they receive a large sum of
money if they lose their job

> A: I'm going to open a bottle of champagne to celebrate. My
> company has just been bought by another one and I'm going
> to lose my job.
>
> B: But that's awful. Why are you celebrating?
>
> A: Because I've got a *golden parachute*. When I leave at the end
> of the week I'll receive a huge cheque!

This expression is a variation on **golden handshake** which was first used in the 1950s
to describe a gift of money given by a company to an employee when he left the
company or retired. In the Eighties *golden parachute* was invented to describe special
contracts for executives who wanted protection if they lost their job—and high
salary!

headhunt   *verb*

fill a vacancy for a job by directly approaching someone who is already working for
another company

> A: I'm worried about my job. All the people who have held this
> post before me have been *headhunted*.
>
> B: Why are you worried? All people who are good at their job
> are *headhunted*.
>
> A: Yes I know. The problem is that I've been working here for
> five years and not a single *headhunter* has approached me!

This expression usually refers to the treatment of very highly paid executives, often
heads of departments within companies. Someone who looks for candidates for
executive jobs is a *headhunter*.

high-flyer

an exceptionally talented professional person who receives rapid promotion

> A: Jamie is a *high-flyer* who works in an advertising company. Last week he announced that he was going to give it all up and become a farmer.
>
> B: I suppose he realised there are more important things than money. When is he leaving the company?
>
> A: He's not. His boss was so worried about losing him that he gave him a £30 000 pay rise and Jamie has decided to stay.

This expression always refers to people who have exceptional ability in a particular field and therefore rise very quickly through an organisation.

See: YUPPIE which describes a professional person who is a potential *high-flyer*.

high-flyer

34

hype   *verb*

over-expose in the media in order to advertise/promote a film, book, person etc

> A: We told the record company that we didn't want them to *hype*
>   our band, 'The Kangaroos'.
>
> B: Yes, *hyping* bands is a complete waste of money. If the music
>   is good enough then people will buy the records. So how
>   many have you sold?
>
> A: None!

This expression originated in America and is thought to be a short form of **hyperbole** which means **deliberate exaggeration**. It can also be used as a noun. For example, *It's amazing the way some people believe the hype about Hollywood films.*

junk food/junk mail   *noun/noun*

unhealthy food which has many additives and high fat content

unwanted post

> A: I've decided to give up *junk food*. I'm going to eat healthy
>   meals instead, lots of fresh vegetables, whole-meal bread
>   and brown rice.
>
> B: Oh dear. Dan and I were going to ask you if you wanted to
>   come with us. We're going out to buy hamburgers with lots of
>   chips. When does your new diet start?
>
> A: Tomorrow!

Junk is another word for **rubbish**. It comes from the Latin word **juncus** meaning **rush,** a type of plant which used to be made into rope. Originally **junk** was used by sailors to describe old pieces of rope, and eventually the word became associated with anything old and generally unwanted. For example, **junk shops** are shops which sell old things which are not very valuable (furniture, clocks, books etc).

Therefore **junk food** is literally **rubbish food**. It is used to describe food which is bought from takeaway shops and supermarkets and eaten with little or no preparation. This type of food usually has very low nutritional value.

A related expression is **junk mail** which describes unwanted post from companies and organisations. If you pick up an envelope which says on the outside *You have won a fantastic prize* or *Open this and find out how you can win £1 million*—it is definitely *junk mail*!

moonlight

moonlight

verb

do another job as well as one's normal one

> A: I don't earn enough money as a nurse so I *moonlight* as a
>   waitress in the evenings.
>
> B: Does it cause any problems?
>
> A: Yes sometimes I get confused. The other day I gave a patient
>   in the hospital a menu and took the temperature of a
>   customer in the restaurant!

This word describes the doing of a second job which is normally secret in some
way—perhaps from the first employer or from the taxman!

36

nightmare scenario

noun

the most awful series of events that can be imagined

> A: I'm very worried about nuclear weapons. If every country has them I don't see how we can avoid the *nightmare scenario* of a world war which destroys the whole Earth. There's only one solution.
>
> B: What's that?
>
> A: Move to another planet!

This expression was first used during the Gulf War in 1991. The Americans and their allies were using military force against Iraq, which had occupied its neighbour Kuwait. According to the Americans, the *nightmare scenario* was the possibility of Iraq retreating very quickly from Kuwait without being defeated. This would mean that the Iraqi army would still be powerful and able to attack again in the future.

sell-by date

noun

the point at which something is no longer at its best and is beginning a natural decline

> A: Most footballers are past their *sell-by date* at thirty-five but Bobby is still a brilliant player. In his last match he scored four times—there was only one problem.
>
> B: What was that?
>
> A: They were own goals!

This term was first used during the early 1970s to indicate when a food product should be sold. The *sell-by date* is printed on edible products in shops so that the consumer can check their freshness. Food which is past its *sell-by date* cannot legally be sold.

Today the expression is also used in a wider, and slightly humorous, way to describe anything which is past its best, or anyone—as in the example above.

squatter

a person who lives in an unused house without the owner's permission and without paying rent

> A: I've been a *squatter* for fifteen years but now I've decided to stop.
>
> B: Is it because you feel that it's immoral to live in someone else's property?
>
> A: No, it's because I've saved so much money through not paying any rent that I can afford to buy a flat of my own now!

The word originated in Australia in the middle of the last century to describe groups of people, generally convicts, who settled in remote areas and claimed the land for themselves. It has commonly been used since the 1970s to describe people living illegally in empty houses. The properties which *squatters* use are nearly always owned by organisations rather than individuals and are often in a state of disrepair.

Other forms are the verb **squat** and the noun **a squat** which refers to the building.

state-of-the-art

adjective

the best technology which is currently available/can be achieved

> A: Do you like my new *state-of-the-art* TV. It has a clock, calendar, radio and video; it tells you the temperature of the room and can even measure your blood pressure. There's just one problem.
>
> B: What's that?
>
> A: I don't know how to turn it on!

This adjective can be used to describe any type of technical or electrical equipment. For example, radios, hi-fi, cameras, televisions, videos, computers, cars, aeroplanes, satellites etc.

the thinking man/woman's   *adjective*

attractive to intellectuals and intelligent people

> **A:** My wife has started watching that TV programme about the history of philosophy.
>
> **B:** My wife likes that too. Personally I find the man who presents it—Professor Peters—very boring, but apparently he's popular.
>
> **A:** I've heard that most of the audience is female so perhaps Professor Peters is *the thinking woman's* sex symbol!

According to the writer Fritz Spiegl, this expression was first used to describe a female English TV presenter. She was called, humorously, **the thinking man's crumpet** (crumpet is slang for attractive woman) which referred to the fact that she was both intelligent and attractive. Now the expression can be used in other forms. For example, *the thinking man's newspaper*.

toyboy   *noun*

boyfriend of an older, usually rich, woman

> **A:** Hello Vera. I've heard that a young man is staying at your house at the moment.
>
> **B:** That's right, his name is Keith and he's staying for the weekend.
>
> **A:** I know you aren't married, Vera, but you must remember that you are over sixty now. Don't you think you're too old to have a *toyboy*?
>
> **B:** *Toyboy*! Keith is my nephew, Mrs Gossip!

This word was invented during the 1980s by the tabloid (popular) newspapers who follow the private lives of the rich and famous. They noticed that many middle-aged film stars had boyfriends who were twenty or thirty years younger than themselves. Because the women paid for everything from meals and clothes to hotels and houses, the tabloids believed that the boyfriends were like possessions or **toys**. Therefore they described the men as *toyboys*.

See: BIMBO which describes a young attractive woman.

user-friendly

user-friendly

adjective

easy to operate/use

> A: We need a new complaints procedure which is simple and clear. Can you think of a *user-friendly* system?
>
> B: Well, at the moment customers have to fill in five different forms which are difficult to understand. How about if they just went to your office and told you about their complaint in person?
>
> A: Oh no, that's too *user-friendly*.

This expression was originally invented to describe a computer which was simple to use and did not need any specialised knowledge. It can be used for machines other than computers, systems (as above) and can even describe people for humorous effect.

This expression inspired the word **ozone-friendly**. It is used by manufacturers to describe products which do not destroy the ozone layer which is the layer of gas around the earth that keeps out most of the harmful rays of the sun. For example, *Is this hairspray ozone-friendly?*

See: DIY which can also describe things which are easy to do.

yuppie
noun

young rich person who works in a well paid job—especially in finance, advertising or marketing

> A: **There's a new shop in the High Street which sells beautiful but very expensive clothes. All the *yuppies* go there.**
>
> B: **How do you know that?**
>
> A: **Because there are always at least two BMWs and one Porsche parked outside!**

Yuppie is an acronym based on 'Young Urban Professional Person'. It was invented in America and became popular in Britain during the 1980s. It's fame spread through such books as 'The Yuppie Handbook' which described this social group and its status symbols.

A *yuppie* is said to like to drive a VW Golf GTi, BMW or Porsche, write with a Mont Blanc pen, visit winebars, carry a Filofax/personal organiser, own a mobile telephone, wear a Rolex watch and designer clothes, be a member of a health club and go on skiing holidays every winter!

The word can also be used as an adjective. For example, *This part of London is a very yuppie area.*

See: HIGH-FLYER which describes a professional person who is very successful.

yuppie

HUMOROUS IDIOMS

When you are tired of trying to learn new vocabulary, look at
this section. It brings together expressions which look and
sound ridiculous—mumbo-jumbo, fuddy-duddy, chock-a-
block! However they are real words and some of them can even
be used in quite formal written English such as articles, reports
or essays.

chock-a-block	mumbo-jumbo
claptrap	namby-pamby
ding-dong	pooh-pooh
fuddy-duddy	riff-raff
gobbledegook	slapdash
hotchpotch	tit for tat
humdrum	topsy-turvy
hurly-burly	whodunnit

chock-a-block

completely full/squashed together in a limited space

> A: Excuse me, I want to get past. I must get to the platform.
>
> B: Don't bother. It's *chock-a-block* with passengers because there's a delay. Apparently the train can't leave the station.
>
> A: Yes I know. I'm the train driver!

This expression originates from nautical slang. The word **chock** refers to a ring-like device through which ropes are passed and **block** refers to two pieces or blocks of wood which are pulled together. They are both part of a block and tackle, a mechanism which is used on ships to hoist or lift heavy loads.

chock-a-block

claptrap *noun*

insincere, foolish talk/nonsense

> A: **What do you think of Linda's painting?**
>
> B: **I like it. She said that she used only blue paint in order to indicate a sad, lonely mood. It's a very clever idea.**
>
> A: **Don't listen to that *claptrap*. Linda used blue paint because it was the only colour she had!**

This word comes from the theatre of the early 18th century. It referred to any trick that the playwright used to make the audience clap—in other words **a trap for claps!** Today it has completely lost its theatrical associations and is only used to describe opinions or information which give the impression of being important but are in fact worthless.

See: MUMBO-JUMBO which can describe meaningless ideas and beliefs as well as language.

GOBBLEDEGOOK which describes complicated language which is difficult to understand.

ding-dong *noun*

loud argument

> A: **Maureen and Richard are having a *ding-dong*. Richard wants to keep a pet and Maureen says that their flat is too small. They've been shouting at each other for over an hour.**
>
> B: **I think Maureen is being unreasonable, they must have room for a pet. What does he want—a cat?**
>
> A: **No, an elephant!**

This slang expression refers to arguments which are very loud and possibly physically violent. It cannot be used to describe a minor disagreement with someone.

fuddy-duddy ⚠   *noun*

someone or something which is very old-fashioned/conservative/boring

> A: **I'd like to buy a suit please. It's for my new job in an accounts department.**
>
> B: **Here's a grey one, Sir, and it's in the latest fashion— everyone's wearing them.**
>
> A: **Oh dear, that's not quite what I had in mind. I hope you don't think I'm a *fuddy-duddy* but do you have anything <u>without</u> orange and purple spots!**

In the past, men who worked in the church were often qualified as Doctors of Philosophy as well as Doctors of Divinity. If a man were both, the letters after his name were PhD, DD. Naturally a clergyman was very conservative in his behaviour and attitudes and so the letters PhD, DD led to the invention of the word *fuddy-duddy*. It is important to remember that it is not regarded as a compliment!

fuddy-duddy

45

gobbledegook

gobbledegook
noun

complicated/obscure/meaningless language (written or spoken)

> A: **My solicitor has sent me a letter which says something about £450! The problem is that he's used so much jargon I can't understand it. I really hate *gobbledegook*—can you help?**
>
> B: **Yes of course. I used to be a solicitor myself so I'm sure I can tell you what it means. Let's see ... Yes, he says that you owe him £450.**
>
> A: **Are you sure? Oh dear. I don't want to understand *gobbledegook*.**

This word was invented by Maury Maverick, an American politician. He was very tired of language which was unnecessarily complicated and hard to understand and so decided to think of a name to describe it. In English the sound a turkey makes is **gobble** and the image of this stupid bird making a sound no one can understand gave Maverick the idea for gobbledegook.

See: MUMBO-JUMBO which can describe meaningless ideas and beliefs as well as language.

CLAPTRAP which describes foolish talk.

46

hotchpotch

noun

a mixture of different things or ideas which do not go together

> **A:** I hate writing reports but my boss says I should do more. What do you think of the latest one I've done?
>
> **B:** To be honest it's a *hotchpotch* of ideas and opinions. I don't think your boss will like it at all.
>
> **A:** That's wonderful. It means she'll never ask me to write one again!

The origin of the word is **hotchpot** which comes from the French **hochepot** which was used to describe a dish made of a mixture of lots of different ingredients. An alternative form of this word is **hodgepodge** which has an identical meaning.

humdrum

adjective

boring/ordinary/repetitive

> **A:** Betty Boring leads a really *humdrum* life. She spends twelve hours a day at the factory, putting chocolates into boxes. At the weekends she stays at home and watches television all day.
>
> **B:** That sounds very depressing. Why does she look so happy all the time?
>
> **A:** Betty says it's because she's a *humdrum* person.

The origin of this word is a mystery but it is thought to have a connection with **hum** which can describe a **continuous unchanging sound** and therefore imply that something is monotonous or uninteresting.

hurly-burly

noun

intense, noisy activity

> A: My grandmother goes to Morello Market every day. She's there when it opens and doesn't leave until it closes.
>
> B: Yes I've heard that it's a very good market. It's very busy with lots of stalls selling everything from food to antiques. Does your grandmother go early so that she can buy the best things?
>
> A: No she doesn't buy anything. She only goes because she enjoys the *hurly-burly*!

This expression is based on the word **hurling** (now meaning **throwing with force**) which once described the sound of thunder and strong wind. It was originally rhymed with the nonsense word **burling** in the phrase **hurling and burling** before it developed to its present form.

Hurly-burly is normally used to describe a busy, active atmosphere which is caused by the presence of lots of people, for example, *the hurly-burly of London*. It cannot be used to describe intense activity carried out by one person.

See: BROUHAHA which also describes noisy activity.

mumbo-jumbo

noun

language, ideas, beliefs which are either too complicated and difficult to understand or nonsensical

> A: I met a scientist last week who explained Einstein's 'Theory of Relativity' to me.
>
> B: I've always been interested in that. What's it all about then?
>
> A: I don't know. He talked a lot of *mumbo-jumbo* about space and time and I didn't understand a word!

When British merchants visited West Africa in the 18th century, they discovered tribes who worshipped a god called **Mama Dyumbo**. Because they didn't believe in the god themselves, the merchants thought that the Africans' religion was silly and meaningless. They called it **mumbo-jumbo** (their pronunciation of Mama Dyumbo) and the expression became part of the English language.

See: GOBBLEDEGOOK which can also describe meaningless language, but not ideas or beliefs.

CLAPTRAP which describes foolish talk.

namby-pamby ⚠

adjective

weak sentimental

> A: My boyfriend says that he wants me to give up smoking. He says that I must choose between him and cigarettes. Do you think he'd be happy if I just smoked less?
>
> B: No, I don't think so. You need to be brave and make a clear decision. It's no good being *namby-pamby*.
>
> A: Yes you're right. I'll tell my boyfriend that I can't see him anymore!

Ambrose Phillips was an 18th century writer and politician who liked to write poetry. Unfortunately he was not very good! Another writer, called Henry Carey, gave Ambrose the nickname **Namby-Pamby** after he wrote a very sentimental poem for Lord Carteret's children. Over the years the nickname has become part of the English language and can be used to describe a person or action which is feeble.

pooh-pooh

verb

completely turn down/treat with contempt an idea or suggestion without further consideration or discussion

> A: I asked my parents if I could go to Australia with my friends but they *pooh-poohed* the idea. They said that I wasn't old enough to travel so far on my own.
>
> B: How did you change their mind?
>
> A: I told them I'd pay for the trip myself!

One of the first known appearances of this word was in Shakespeare's play, 'Hamlet' in the form **puh**: 'Affection, puh! You speake like a greene girle.'

During the 17th century the word became a double word—*pooh-pooh*—in order to provide greater emphasis.

riff-raff

undesirable and untrustworthy people who are of a low social class

> A: **Would you like to go to the Queen's Head pub?**
>
> B: **I don't think so. It seems to attract all kinds of *riff-raff*. Why on earth do you want to go?**
>
> A: **I'm meeting my friends there!**

This word is normally used to refer to a group of people. Its origin is the Old French expression **rif et raf** which meant everyone/one and all.

slapdash

adjective

inefficient/of a low standard

> A: **I paid two decorators to paint my flat. What do you think?**
>
> B: **It looks like a really *slapdash* job to me—I think you should ask for your money back. They obviously aren't very experienced.**
>
> A: **But they must have lots of experience—they are both over ninety years old!**

This word is based on the phrase **a slap and a dash**. The verbs **slap** and **dash** both indicate hurry and communicate the idea of not being careful.

slapdash

tit for tat

an unpleasant action given in return for one received

> A: **Andrew was furious when I got the job which he wanted. He came round to my house with a ladder in the middle of the night to splash red paint over my windows.**
>
> B: **That's outrageous. If I were you I would go round to his house and pour paint over his car.**
>
> A: **No, I don't believe in *tit for tat*. Anyway Andrew fell off the ladder and broke his leg—so now he's even more angry!**

In the 16th century **tip** and **tap** both meant a **hit** or a **blow**. The expression **tip for tap** therefore meant a **blow in exchange for a blow**. Over the time the spelling has altered to the current *tit for tat*.

topsy-turvy

adjective

chaotic/upside down

reversed/having changed places

> A: **When we returned home from holiday last night we found everything was *topsy-turvy*. Books and furniture had been thrown around, plates and glasses had been smashed—the flat was a complete mess.**
>
> B: **Oh my goodness, you must tell the police immediately that you've been burgled.**
>
> A: **But it wasn't a burglary. Our daughter had thrown a party for her friends while we were away!**

This expression comes from two words, **top** and the Old English verb **terve** which meant **turn** or **turn over**.

It was used by Charles Dickens in one of his stories: 'A chaos of carts, overthrown and jumbled together lay topsy-turvy at the bottom of a . . . hill.'

Apart from describing confusion and disorder, the word can also be used to refer to two things which have reversed their position, for example, *I dreamt that I was in a topsy-turvy world last night. The sky was green and the grass and trees were blue.*

whodunnit

a detective novel or play

> A: My Aunt Nellie loves to read *whodunnits* so I send her an Agatha Christie each birthday. She's read about so many murders over the years she must be an expert by now.
>
> B: Yes I'm sure. How is her husband, Uncle George? Do you send him presents as well?
>
> A: Now that's strange. You know I haven't heard from him for ages!

This expression is an abbreviation of the question **'Who has done it?'** This of course means **'Who did the murder?'** All crime novels and plays contain this puzzle which the reader attempts to solve.

whodunnit

FOREIGN IDIOMS

One of the reasons why there are so many words in the English language is that a large number of them are 'borrowed' from other languages. These expressions have been absorbed to become part of the English vocabulary. However, you will find that all the pronunciations are 'anglicised'—in other words they are spoken with an English accent, as if they are English words.

ad nauseam

au fait

bête noire

blasé

blitz

brouhaha

carte blanche

cliché/clichéd

crème de la crème

faux pas

forte

kowtow

macho

paparazzi

per se

pièce de resistance

post mortem

raconteur

status quo

tête-à-tête

ad nauseam

endlessly/in excess/too much

> A: **The English are lucky that they have such bad weather.**
>
> B: **Why is that?**
>
> A: **Because it's the only subject they can talk about—they discuss it *ad nauseam*!**

This Latin expression literally means **to the point of sickness**. It is important to remember that it generally refers to something which is unpleasant. For example, *I love oysters. I could eat them ad nauseam.*—is wrong; but, *No one in my family likes sausages but they're all my mother can cook. We eat them ad nauseam.*—is right.

au fait

/əʊ ˈfeɪ/ *adjective*

knowledgeable about a subject or situation

> A: **Doctor Quack told me he was *au fait* with the latest medical discoveries and so I thought he would give me something very special to stop my earache.**
>
> B: **I never go to Doctor Quack when I'm ill. I've heard that he isn't a qualified doctor at all, but a greengrocer.**
>
> A: **Really? So that's why he gave me a bag of apples instead of some medicine!**

This French expression is used to describe knowing **about** something rather than knowing **how to do** something. There are two ways it can be used. First, when referring to someone who has great knowledge about a topic or subject—for example, *Henry is au fait with American law*. Second, when describing someone who is simply aware of a situation—for example, *Are you au fait with what has happened?*

bête noire

bête noire

/bet ˈnwɑː/*noun*

something or someone one hates/detests

> A: **Gardening never stops; every day something has to be done—weeding, pruning, digging, planting . . .**
>
> B: **Yes, I can see you work really hard; the garden looks beautiful.**
>
> A: **Actually gardening is my *bête noire* so I never do any. I pay my gardener, Mr Rake, to do it all for me!**

This expression literally means **black beast** in French. The plural form in English is *bête noires*.

blasé

/ˈblɑːzeɪ/ *adjective*

unmoved/unexcited by something because one has experienced it many times already

> A: I find it difficult to choose a holiday. I travel abroad as part of my job so flying to America or the Far East is like driving to the shops for me.
>
> B: Yes I see what you mean. Visiting so many exotic countries would make anyone *blasé*. So where do you go?
>
> A: I've found a unique holiday destination which only I know about. I stay with my mother down the road!

This word comes from the French verb **blaser** which means **cloy** (become unpleasant because of having too much of something). It was originally used to describe people who are bored with something because they have experienced it many times before. However the meaning has expanded and the word can also refer to someone who is unimpressed by something even if it is a first time experience. For example, *I thought my young son would find his first visit to the circus exciting but he was very blasé about it.*

See: CLICHÉ which describes something which has been overused.

blitz

/blɪts/ *noun*

intensive effort or fierce attack

> A: I decided to have a *blitz* on my clothes and threw away all the ones I didn't want any more. It's not something I'm going to do again for a very long time . . .
>
> B: Why? Because it took hours to do?
>
> A: No. Because it was so expensive. When I'd finished I found I didn't have anything left except a pair of socks—so I had to go out and buy a whole new wardrobe!

This is the shortened form of the German word **Blitzkrieg** which means literally **lightning war**. It was used during the Second World War to describe the intensive air attacks carried out on Britain. The British adopted the word and called the attacks 'The Blitz'. After the war, the word came to be used to describe any fierce, concentrated effort.

It can also be used as a verb. For example, *The government are going to blitz small businesses with information about fire regulations.*

brouhaha   /'bruːhaːhaː/ *noun*

loud noises due to intense activity or a long and heated argument

> A: What's the matter with Harry? He's in such a bad mood.
>
> B: Oh, there's been a bit of a *brouhaha* because I left a tube of glue in the bathroom.
>
> A: What's so awful about that?
>
> B: He mistook it for toothpaste and brushed his teeth with it!

This French word imitates a loud noise: it sounds like the noise it is describing. The use of the sound of a word to imitate what the word refers to is called onomatopoeia. **Hiss** and **buzz** are other examples of onomatopoeia.

See: HURLY-BURLY which also describes intense noisy activity.

carte blanche   /kaːt ˈblaːnʃ/ *noun*

freedom to decide everything/anything

> A: The new art gallery is certain to look awful. I've heard that the architects, 'Devastating Designs', have been given *carte blanche*.
>
> B: Some modern architecture is very attractive—so it might not look as bad as you think. What was their last building like?
>
> A: A rabbit hutch!

This French expression literally means **blank sheet of paper**. It originated from the military tradition of giving a blank piece of paper to the leader of a beaten army. The leader had to sign his name on the paper so that the victors could write above it all the conditions which they wanted. Obviously anything could be written so the defeated side were giving the victors *carte blanche*.

carte blanche

57

cliché/clichéd

an idea/expression/action which is unoriginal/overused

> A: **I only work in an office, but I've always wanted to be one of those filmstars and go to glamorous parties every night. It must be wonderful living in Hollywood. I really envy them.**
>
> B: **That's a very *clichéd* image. Actually most stars stay at home in the evening and go to bed early because they have to be on the filmset by six in the morning.**
>
> A: **Well in that case they probably envy me!**

This French word can be either used as a noun or an adjective. For example, *Your schooldays are the happiest days of your life* is a *cliché* or *The film had a clichéd ending*.

See: BLASÉ which describes the attitude of someone who experiences something so many times they feel it is clichéd.

CORNY which also means unoriginal but in a sentimental way.

crème de la crème

/krem də læ ˈkrem/ *noun*

the very best/the élite

> A: **My friend Doris is going to the Garden Party at Buckingham Palace. The *crème de la crème* will be there—Lords, Ladies, Dukes and Duchesses—it'll be so exciting.**
>
> B: **How did she get an invitation? Doris works in a hotel kitchen; she's not a Duchess.**
>
> A: **They asked her to make the cucumber sandwiches!**

This French expression means **cream of the cream**. The cream is the best part of the milk and therefore the cream of the cream is the absolute best. The expression can be used to describe objects or people. If you look in *The Times* newspaper you will find a job section called 'Crème de la Crème'. It advertises very highly paid secretarial jobs.

faux pas

/fəʊ ˈpɑː/ *noun*

embarrassing social mistake

> A: I had a drink with our new neighbour, Mrs Zambuni. We talked about all sorts of things, even politics. I said that all politicians were liars and should be put in prison!
>
> B: Oh dear you've made a huge *faux pas*. Her father has been a Member of Parliament for twenty-five years!

Meaning **false step**, this French expression only describes mistakes which are made in a social situation, for example, at a meeting or party.

forte

/ˈfɔːteɪ/ *noun*

strength/talent

> A: I'm arranging a retirement party for my father who's sixty-five this month but I'm very worried he won't enjoy it.
>
> B: Leave it to me—parties are my *forte*. All we need to do is provide music, food and alcohol and avoid anything he doesn't like. What things does your father hate the most?
>
> A: Music, food and alcohol!

This Italian word, meaning **strong**, is used as a word for someone's most outstanding ability.

forte

kowtow

behave humbly and obey someone without question

> A: **My boss expects me to *kowtow* to him all the time. The other day he dropped an envelope on the floor and told me to pick it up. I was so angry I told him to do it himself so he picked it up and locked it in his desk.**
>
> B: **Well done. I'm sure that taught him a lesson.**
>
> A: **And me. My wages were in that envelope!**

This expression was brought back from China by early European explorers. It comes from the two Mandarin words **kou** (strike) and **tou** (head). The literal meaning is **kneel down before a superior and touch the ground with one's head.** Today the expression implies that someone's behaviour is too meek or humble so it cannot be used as a compliment!

See: EAT HUMBLE PIE which has a similar meaning but although both expressions describe humble behaviour there is one important difference. If you eat humble pie you are regretting a previous action. If you *kowtow* there is not a clearly defined reason for acting humbly.

macho

aggressively masculine

> A: **My husband said he wouldn't help with the housework because it wasn't *macho*. I was very surprised because I didn't think he worried about that sort of thing.**
>
> B: **If a man has a very masculine job—like being a lorry driver—he can feel silly doing things which are traditionally associated with women.**
>
> A: **Yes I know what you mean, but my husband is a ballet dancer!**

This is a Mexican–Spanish word derived from the Latin, **masculus**, meaning simply **male.** However, American journalists in the late 1950s began to use the word to suggest excessive or aggressive maleness and this is the meaning it now holds in English. The noun is **machismo**.

paparazzi

showbusiness photographers who follow the rich and famous anywhere to get a good picture

> **A:** Mr Feature, there are dozens of *paparazzi* outside the restaurant. Could I suggest you leave by the back door?
>
> **B:** Thank you, waiter. I must admit it's such a bore to find one's photo on the front page of the newspapers.
>
> **A:** Actually sir, they're waiting for Miss Blockbuster at the next table. She told me that she's happy for them to take photos of her but she doesn't want you to get in the way!

This type of photo-journalism was invented by Italian photographers in Rome who waited outside fashionable night clubs and restaurants. The idea was to take photographs of celebrities unexpectedly and without their permission in order to get unusual pictures to sell to magazines and newspapers. The word **paparazzi** means **buzzing insects** and indicates the annoyance which the photographers cause their victims.

per se

/pɜː 'seɪ/

when considered without taking other factors into account

> **A:** It's not that I want to leave home *per se*, Mother. I promise you I've always been very content here.
>
> **B:** Then why are you going? We've always let you bring friends round, play music in your room and even stay out late.
>
> **A:** Yes I know, but this morning we received a letter which said our house was going to be knocked down to make way for a motorway!

This Latin expression is normally used with a negative, as in the example above. It indicates that you are about to explain the additional factors which alter a situation. A common way of using it is to qualify an assumed disadvantage or negative judgement. For example, *I'm sorry we can't give you a job. It's not that your are too expensive per se, it's rather that the company cannot afford to take on new staff at the moment.*

pièce de resistance

/ˈpies də reˈzɪstɑːns/*noun*

the best one of several similar things which someone has made/done/created

> A: **Lily has redecorated the whole house. Every room now has new curtains, carpets and wallpaper but the *pièce de resistance* is definitely the garage.**
>
> B: **What has she done to it—given it a new coat of paint?**
>
> A: **No, she's converted it into a swimming pool!**

This French phrase was originally an artistic expression for the best piece of work (painting, sculpture etc) in a series. However in English it can be used to describe any type of object in a collection, for example, the best dish in a meal or the best song in an opera.

post mortem

/pəʊst ˈmɔːtəm/*noun*

analysis/examination of an event which has happened

> A: **When I lost the tennis match my coach wanted a *post mortem*. I would have liked to forget all about it and concentrate on my next match.**
>
> B: **It's a good idea to discuss your mistakes. I'm sure the *post mortem* helped you. What did your coach say?**
>
> A: **She advised me to give up tennis entirely!**

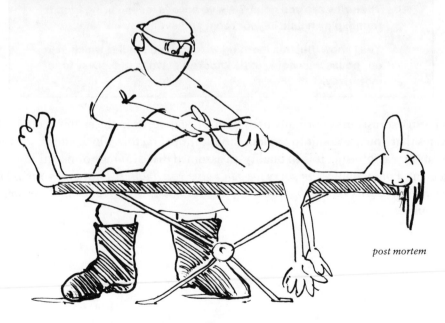

post mortem

This Latin phrase means **after death**. When a doctor examines a dead body to find out the cause of death he carries out a **post mortem** but the phrase is now commonly used in many other situations as well. Because of its original meaning however, it usually refers to events which are unpleasant.

raconteur
/rækɒn'tɜː/*noun*

a person who is good at telling long, interesting, amusing stories or anecdotes

> A: **Most people prefer listening to the sound of their own voice rather than other people's.**
>
> B: **Yes, that's true. That's why I always say that if someone else tells a very long story they are a bore, but if you tell one yourself then you're a *raconteur*!**

Raconteur originates from the French verb **raconter** which means **tell**. It is regarded as a great compliment if you call someone a *raconteur* so be sure they deserve it!

status quo
/steɪtəs 'kwəʊ/*noun*

the current or existing situation/harmony

> A: **Some Londoners moved to the small village of Brightly because they didn't like the unfriendly atmosphere of a big city.**
>
> B: **I've heard that people who live in the country don't like strangers. They prefer to maintain the *status quo*. So how did the villagers react to the new arrivals?**
>
> A: **They were so unfriendly that after six months the Londoners decided to move back to the capital again!**

This Latin expression is always used with **the** (*the status quo*) and refers to situations which have existed unchanged for a long time. It usually describes situations which are stable, calm and harmonious. For example, *The revolution disturbed the status quo on the small island*. The most commonly used phrases are: *keep/maintain/preserve the status quo* and *disturb/change/alter the status quo*.

tête-à-tête

a private/intimate conversation between just two people

> **A:** I don't like Chris—he has no sense of humour.
>
> **B:** That's rubbish. I saw you having a *tête-à-tête* with him last night. You looked really amused.
>
> **A:** Yes I know. Just before he sat down next to me I noticed there was a great lump of chewing gum on the chair!

This French expression literally means **head to head**. It describes the tendency for two people to lean their heads near to each other when talking so that others cannot hear.

tête-à-tête

SLANG

'Slang' is not thought of as proper English but everyone uses it! It is most popular as a spoken rather than a written language and generally used in informal situations. It is only safe to use 'slang' with friends or people you know very well.

Two expressions in this section (*rabbit* and *have a butchers*) are cockney rhyming slang. This used to be a secret language in the East End of London. It was spoken by criminals who didn't want other people to find out about their illegal plans and activities. Some of the expressions eventually became so popular that they began to be used by everybody.

be bunged up
bonkers
booze
bumf
burn oneself out
clapped-out
corny
duff someone up
five o'clock shadow
flog
gunge
have a butchers at something

iffy
kick the bucket
old banger
plonk
put a sock in it
rabbit
rip someone off/a rip-off
spare tyre
tear someone off a strip
wet blanket
whinge
wind someone up

be bunged up
verb

be unable to breathe properly due to a cold

> A: Doctor, I'm very ill—please help me. I have a bad headache, a high temperature, I*'m bunged up* and I'm tired all the time.
>
> B: This is obviously your first visit to Britain.
>
> A: Why do you say that?
>
> B: Because if you had been here before you'd know that all you have is a British cold!

A **bung** is a stopper (like a cork in a wine bottle) and so *bunged up* is another expression for **blocked up**. The phrase can be used to describe anything which is blocked. For example, *the drain is bunged up*. However when applied to people it refers to the cold symptom of being unable to breathe properly.

bonkers ⚠
adjective

mad or crazy; very excited

> A: Alison is going to spend the next twelve months travelling around the world.
>
> B: What a great idea. Are you going to go with her?
>
> A: No, certainly not, I think she's *bonkers*. She's travelling the whole way on a bicycle!

The example illustrates one meaning of the word. The second meaning, **very excited**, is used in the phrase **go bonkers**. For example, *All the Italians went bonkers when they won the football match*.

booze

alcoholic drink

> A: **We have to go through customs when we land. Do you have much to declare?**
>
> B: **No, nothing.**
>
> A: **What about all that *booze* you bought?**
>
> B: **I've put it in your suitcase!**

This word can also be used as a verb. **To booze** means to drink too much. Another related word is **boozer**. This can mean a **pub** or a **heavy drinker**.

bumf

bumf

printed information/advertisements/brochures (often unwanted)

> A: **The estate agent sent me some *bumf* about a house. It said it was 'uniquely situated' so I went to see it.**
>
> B: **That sounds very interesting. What was so unique about its situation then?**
>
> A: **It was next to a motorway!**

This word was originally 19th-century slang for toilet paper. Today it still has a connection with paper although now it refers to documents, brochures or leaflets of all kinds. Despite its past it is not an impolite word and can be used in any circumstances!

burn oneself out

use up all one's energy over a long period

> A: Miss Williams, I think you're working far too hard. You arrive at the office no later than 8 o'clock every morning. If you're not careful you'll *burn yourself out*.
>
> B: But I enjoy my work Mr Meaney, so I don't mind long hours.
>
> A: Well in that case, would you mind coming in at 7 o'clock from now on? I'm sure I can find you lots more work to do!

This expression is normally used to describe using up too much energy through overwork and implies that someone is trying to achieve too much too soon. It is important to remember that one cannot *burn oneself out* in an hour or an afternoon; it must take place over a long time—weeks, months or years.

See: CLAPPED-OUT which means worn out, exhausted.

clapped-out ⚠

old, worn-out and possibly broken (object)

very tired, worn-out (person)

> A: Did you have a nice holiday?
>
> B: Not really. Every day my boyfriend insisted that we swim twenty lengths before breakfast, run ten miles before lunch and walk for three hours in the mountains in the afternoon. I feel really *clapped-out*.
>
> A: Yes, you do look rather pale and tired. What you need is a holiday—only next time remember to leave your boyfriend behind!

This expression can be used to describe either objects, such as cars, bicycles, watches etc, or less usually, people. When using it for describing objects be careful not to use it simply as a substitute for **broken** as it can only refer to things which are old. So, *My new car has broken down—it's clapped out* is wrong. But, *My old car keeps breaking down—it's clapped-out* is right. If using it to describe a person, it is important to be aware that it is not very polite.

See: BURN ONESELF OUT which can be used to describe using up all one's energy over a long period.

corny

unoriginal due to being overused and sentimental

> A: I've written a short story but I don't know how to end it. I was thinking of making the two main characters get married and live happily ever after.
>
> B: Oh no, that's a really *corny* ending—it's been done a hundred times before.
>
> A: Not by me—it's my first story!

This word originally described rural American audiences with simple, unsophisticated tastes. Because the farmers grew corn, they were known as **corn-fed** and the humour they liked came to be known as *corny*. Today you can use the word to describe many things. For example, *corny jokes, corny films, corny tastes*.

See: CLICHÉ which also describes something which is unoriginal.

duff someone up
verb

hit someone many times/beat someone up

> A: Muggerstown is the most dangerous place in the world. I really worry about the old ladies who live here. If you walk along a dark street late at night, you're almost certain to get *duffed up*.
>
> B: Yes, but most big cities have that sort of problem. Why do you think Muggerstown is so bad?
>
> A: Because it's the old ladies who *duff people up*!

This expression is used to describe violence which is quite severe but not extreme or fatal. It can be used in the making of humorous threats, for example, *If you don't shut up, I'll come over there and duff you up*.

five o'clock shadow

noun

the beard which grows in a day after a man shaves in the morning

> A: **My beard grows faster than other men's.**
>
> B: **How do you know that?**
>
> A: **Because I always get a *five o'clock shadow* by two in the afternoon!**

The word **shadow** refers to the way in which a slight growth of beard turns a man's chin slightly blue.

five o'clock shadow

flog

verb

sell

> A: **I've got good news and bad news. The good news is that I managed to sell your old desk to the antique shop for a hundred pounds.**
>
> B: **That's great. What's the bad news?**
>
> A: **I was in the shop this afternoon and saw the dealer *flog* it to a customer for a thousand!**

Flog can also mean **beat or whip harshly and persistently**. The meaning of **sell** derives from the same idea of extreme persistence. In other words, someone who *flogs* something is trying hard to be persuasive and will probably never give up.

gunge *noun*

a sticky mess

> A: **The meal was fantastic until the last course. We were given some brown *gunge* in a glass that looked and tasted like mud.**
>
> B: **What was it?**
>
> A: **I hope I never find out!**

This word can be used to describe any unpleasant substance which is half-way between a liquid and a solid. It is thought that it may have derived from a combination of the word **goo**, a sticky substance, and **sponge**, a squashy, damp substance.

have a butchers at something *verb*

look

> A: **Can I *have a butchers at the newspaper*? That one has lots of interesting stories about people's private lives. I love reading gossip.**
>
> B: **I don't think you should look at it.**
>
> A: **Why not?**
>
> B: **Because it's got a picture of you on the front page!**

This expression comes from cockney rhyming slang. The original phrase is **butcher's hook** which rhymes with **look**. It is always used in its shortened form.

gone off/rotten (food)

> A: I'm worried about the fish we ate last night.
>
> B: Yes it did smell *iffy*, but when you gave it to the cat he liked it. Animals always know if food is safe to eat so what's the problem?
>
> A: The cat's just died!

stolen (goods)

> A: I was offered a Rolex watch by a friend for only £50. It's definitely a real one so I'm thinking of buying it.
>
> B: Don't! If it's that cheap and it's not an imitation, it must be *iffy*. What is this friend of yours like?
>
> A: I don't know much about him. He's just come out of prison!

dishonest/almost illegal (action)

> A: Eric has opened fifty bank accounts all over the country. He says it will mean that he'll pay less tax.
>
> B: That sounds a bit *iffy* to me. Surely one person isn't allowed to have so many accounts.
>
> A: It's all right—they're all in different names!

This flexible word can be used in three different ways—however, they all have the meaning **not acceptable** in common. Its origin probably lies with the word **if** which implies doubt and uncertainty—a characteristic of all the above meanings.

kick the bucket ⚠ *verb*

die

> A: I'd like to live to one hundred years old.
>
> B: It's not that difficult. You just have to be careful about what you eat—no meat, alcohol or chocolates—and take plenty of exercise.
>
> A: If that's the only way to do it I think I'd prefer to eat what I want, not take any exercise and *kick the bucket* at sixty!

This expression is always thought of as humorous and is generally used to make people laugh. However the two theories to explain its origin are not funny at all! The first theory is that the phrase comes from the old method of killing pigs at a market. The dead animal would be hung upside down and its feet tied to a length of wood known as a **bucket**. The pig's feet would therefore knock or **kick** against the **bucket**. The other theory comes from a method of committing suicide by standing on a bucket with a noose of rope around the neck. The person **kicked the bucket** away in order to hang himself. You can decide which you think sounds more believable!

old banger
noun

an old, dirty car which is almost worn-out

> **A:** I have to visit my mother every month. She lives in the country and it takes hours to travel there by train.
>
> **B:** Why don't you buy yourself an *old banger*—it wouldn't cost very much. Then your journey would be much quicker and easier.
>
> **A:** I don't think that's a good idea. My mother would expect me to visit her every <u>week</u> if I did that!

The expression derives from the fact that an old car often backfires and makes loud **bangs**. It must always be used in its full form because a **banger** without **old** is a slang word meaning sausage!

plonk
noun

cheap wine

> **A:** All the guests had brought superb wines. Some of the vintages were twenty years old.
>
> **B:** What did you take?
>
> **A:** A bottle of *plonk* from the supermarket!

This word is thought to have been invented during the First World War by soldiers who turned the French phrase **vin blanc** (white wine) into the humorous *plonk*. It can be used to describe any wine, red or white, which is not of good quality.

put a sock in it
verb

shut up/quieten down

> A: **My son Jim is going to be an opera singer.**
>
> B: **That's nice. You must feel very proud to have someone musical in the family.**
>
> A: **Not really. He practises every day at 3 in the morning so I'm always telling him to *put a sock in it*!**

This expression is said to come from the time of the gramophone (old-fashioned record player). In its early days there was no way of controlling the volume of the sound which came from a large horn. So the only way to make the noise quieter was to place a sock inside the horn—to *put a sock in it*. Today the expression is used to ask someone to be quiet and one of its most common forms is the exclamation: *Put a sock in it!*

rabbit
verb

talk too much

> A: **My father said he would give my mother £50 if she could keep quiet for half an hour.**
>
> B: **What happened, did she do it?**
>
> A: **Yes, but she was so excited that she'd won, she didn't stop *rabbiting* about it all week!**

The word comes from cockney rhyming slang; **rabbit and pork** means **talk**. It is one of the cockney terms which has become so popular that it has spread into everyday language. Variations are: *rabbit away about something* and *rabbit on about something*.

rip someone off/a rip-off

verb/noun

cheat someone

something which is not worth its price

> A: Do you like my new leather jacket—it cost one thousand pounds.
>
> B: One thousand pounds just for a jacket! That's *a rip-off*.
>
> A: The man in the market said it was the very best quality leather.
>
> B: I know that man—he *rips everybody off*. He should have said 'best quality plastic'. Your jacket isn't even real leather!

The expression can be used as a verb or a noun.

See: PAY THROUGH THE NOSE which also describes paying too much for something.

spare tyre ⚠

noun

excess fat around the waist

> A: Stanley didn't sunbathe during the whole holiday. He said he had forgotten his swimming trunks but that was just an excuse.
>
> B: What was the real reason?
>
> A: He's a little overweight and he didn't want anyone to see his *spare tyre*!

The expression describes the appearance of the layer of fat which develops—usually in middle age—around the waist. The origin of the word is the **spare tyre** which is kept in the boot of a car for emergencies. Obviously the shape and appearance of a rubber tyre is similar to the roll of fat around the waist!

spare tyre

tear someone off a strip

talk to someone angrily

> **A:** The next time I see Charlie I'm going to *tear him off a strip*. I lent him a book called 'Improve Your Memory' and he hasn't given it back. He's had it for over a year now.
>
> **B:** Why doesn't he return it?
>
> **A:** He says he keeps forgetting!

This is based on the Old English verb **tear** which meant **rage/be violently angry**. As is quite common in the evolution of a word, it has become confused with the more modern version, nowadays **tear** means **pull apart/rip**.

wet blanket ⚠
noun

someone who spoils others' fun by being miserable or unenthusiastic

> **A:** No one likes Bill because he's such a *wet blanket*.
>
> **B:** What's wrong with him?
>
> **A:** Well, last time we took him to a disco he complained to the manager that the music was too loud!

wet blanket

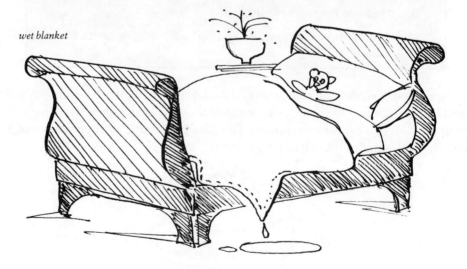

The expression is based on the idea that a **wet blanket** is used to put out fires. Fires represent excitement and passion so a *wet blanket* represents something which is boring and dull.

whinge ⚠   *verb*

complain without good reason/whine

> A: I gave Eric a full-time job in my company. It was a big mistake. This morning he came to see me and *whinged* that working thirty-five hours a week was too much.
>
> B: But thirty-five hours is a normal working week. How many hours does Eric work now?
>
> A: None—I've given him the sack!

This word implies that someone complains over and over again. It also indicates that the person is behaving in an immature way, like a spoilt child—so it is not complimentary!

wind someone up   /waɪnd .../*verb*

tease someone

> A: My goodness, there's a huge black insect on your head. It's got five pairs of eyes and hairy legs.
>
> B: How horrible! Please get it off me! Quickly!
>
> A: No don't worry, I'm *winding you up*. There's nothing there at all!

The expression comes from the action of **winding up** a clock in order to **make it go**. The idea of being in control is carried over to its slang use. One can control or affect the behaviour of a person by *winding him up*.

wind someone up

77

PROVERBS

Proverbs are wise sayings, often warnings, which have been passed from generation to generation. Nobody knows exactly when they were first used or who invented them but their advice will never be out of date. Sometimes a proverb is so well-known that only the first half of it is used—for example, *It's the last straw* instead of *It's the last straw that broke the camel's back*.

You will probably find that you can think of proverbs in your own language which have the same meaning as some of these, but are expressed in a different way. For example, while the English say, *Don't count your chickens before they hatch*, the Germans say, *Don't count your money before you have it*.

a bird in the hand is worth two in the bush
don't count your chickens before they hatch
easier said than done
easy come, easy go
go from the sublime to the ridiculous
it's no use crying over spilt milk
last straw that broke the camel's back (the)
let sleeping dogs lie
once bitten, twice shy
one swallow doesn't make a summer
strike while the iron is hot
there's no smoke without fire
truth is stranger than fiction
you can't have your cake and eat it

a bird in the hand is worth two in the bush

it is foolish to risk everything one has for the possibility of something better

> A: A film director offered me a part in a film. He said it could make me into a star overnight.
>
> B: Take my advice; *a bird in the hand is worth two in the bush*. You have a good office job at the moment—why risk losing that for a film which might not be a success?
>
> A: Because the director is Steven Spielberg!

A common form of this proverb is the phrase, *It's a case of a bird in the hand . . .*

a bird in the hand is worth two in the bush

don't count your chickens (before they hatch)

don't assume a good result before you know there is one

> A: **I've booked a honeymoon for Lisa and myself. We're going to Barbados in the Caribbean.**
>
> B: ***Aren't you counting your chickens before they're hatched?*** **She hasn't even agreed to marry you yet!**

As the expression is so long, it is often shortened to *Don't count your chickens!* especially when used as an exclamation.

See: ONE SWALLOW DOESN'T MAKE A SUMMER which advises caution, even though one good thing has already happened; in the case of *don't count your chickens*, caution is advised and nothing good has happened yet.

don't count your chickens before they hatch

easier said than done

extremely difficult to do

> A: **I've just flown over from America with Confusion Airlines. The flight was a nightmare—everything went wrong.**
>
> B: **Never mind madam, you're here at last in London. The White Horse Hotel will look after you much better. Shall I take your luggage to your room?**
>
> A: **That's *easier said than done*. Thanks to Confusion Airlines my luggage is in Nairobi!**

easy come, easy go

anything which is acquired with little effort can be easily and quickly lost

> A: Yesterday my husband went shopping and spent £50 000 of my money.
>
> B: That's dreadful—you must be really angry with him.
>
> A: Not at all. I won the money at a casino last week so I feel its *easy come, easy go!*

go from the sublime to the ridiculous

move from one situation which is wonderful or perfect to another which is absurd or awful

> A: The ceremony for the coronation was incredible. The King wore beautiful robes and the cathedral was full of people, music and flowers.
>
> B: What happened after he was crowned?
>
> A: It *went from the sublime to the ridiculous*. The King came out of the cathedral and rode back to his palace on a bicycle!

The original proverb was **from the sublime to the ridiculous is only one step.** It is often used in the exclamation, *Talk about going from the sublime to the ridiculous!*

it's no use crying over spilt milk

there's no point in regretting something which cannot be changed

> A: I left the roast chicken on the table for just five minutes, but when I came back the dog had eaten it all. If only I hadn't left it there—it was such a silly thing to do.
>
> B: Look, *there's no use crying over spilt milk*. We'll have something else for dinner instead. What is there in the fridge?
>
> A: Just a tin of dog food!

Common variations of this proverb are *It's no good crying over spilt milk.* or *There's no point crying over spilt milk.* and the command, *Don't cry over spilt milk.*

the last straw (that broke the camel's back)

a final problem or setback which makes a situation completely unbearable

> **A:** I've had very bad luck this year. My wife has left me, my mother has been kidnapped, I've lost my job and my house has been knocked down to make way for a motorway.
>
> **B:** No wonder you look so unhappy.
>
> **A:** Yes, but when my pet mouse died this morning it was *the last straw*!

This saying is often shortened to *the last (or final) straw* or *the straw that broke the camel's back*. It is found in Charles Dickens' book, 'Dombey and Son' in which he wrote 'As the last straw breaks the laden camel's back, this piece of information crushed the sinking spirits of Mr Dombey.'

the last straw that broke the camel's back

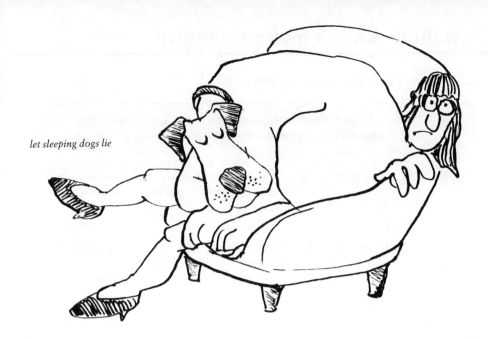

let sleeping dogs lie

let sleeping dogs lie

do not interfere with or change something which may cause problems if it is
disturbed or alerted

> A: I knew the hotel was haunted but I didn't tell Jerry. I thought it
>   was best to *let sleeping dogs lie*.
>
> B: Yes of course, he might have been very frightened by the
>   thought of ghosts.
>
> A: Not at all—that's the problem. He would have spent the
>   whole night trying to find them and disturbing all the guests!

once bitten, twice shy

reluctant to repeat an action or experience which has had an unpleasant result in the
past

> A: Why don't you bet on Golden Lad—he's a wonderful horse?
>   I'm putting £50 on him because I'm sure he'll win.
>
> B: It's a case of *once bitten, twice shy*. You told me to bet on
>   Blue Lightning last week and he came last.
>
> A: Yes I know, but he did very well for a horse with only three
>   legs!

one swallow doesn't make a summer

one success doesn't guarantee complete success

> **A:** Today a woman telephoned to ask me to design her wedding dress. She said she wanted it to be the most luxurious and lavish creation I could think of.
>
> **B:** That's fantastic—your first order! I know *one swallow doesn't make a summer* but I'm sure your fashion business will soon take off now. So have you started work on this incredible dress?
>
> **A:** No. When I told her how much it would cost, she said she'd buy one from the local department store instead!

This proverb is based on the fact that swallows (a type of bird) migrate to Britain for the summer—therefore their arrival is a sign that the season has started. However, the proverb warns that you must not assume that it is summer just because you see one swallow—there have to be lots of them! **One swallow** is a metaphor for **one good thing or sign** and **summer** is a metaphor for **complete success**.

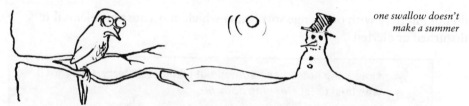

one swallow doesn't make a summer

See: DON'T COUNT YOUR CHICKENS BEFORE THEY HATCH which also advises caution.

strike while the iron is hot

act immediately to take advantage of an ideal situation

> **A:** I've been thinking of asking John to marry me for weeks. Today he seems to be in a really good mood so I'm going to *strike while the iron is hot*. By the way, do you know why he's so happy at the moment?
>
> **B:** Yes, I'm afraid I do. You see John proposed to me this morning and I accepted. We're going to be married in the spring!

This proverb comes from the blacksmiths' profession. Blacksmiths make metal **shoes** and nail them to horses' hooves. As the horseshoe needs to be a perfect fit, it is heated in a fire and then hit with a hammer to make the right shape. Obviously the metal must be hit while it is still hot and easy to bend.

there's no smoke without fire

there is always some truth in a rumour

> A: My neighbour says 96-year-old Mr Batty is leaving his whole fortune to his cat, but I don't believe it.
>
> B: I agree it seems ridiculous, but *there's no smoke without fire*.
>
> A: That's true. Actually, I've got two cats myself. Do you think if I introduce them to Mr Batty, he might leave some money to them too?

truth is stranger than fiction

real life can be more incredible than anything which can be imagined

> A: Do you remember that I lost my ring? Well, it's been found.
>
> B: I don't believe it. You dropped it over the edge of a boat and it fell into the sea.
>
> A: Yes I know, but *truth is stranger than fiction*. Our neighbour likes to go fishing and yesterday he caught an enormous cod. When he cut it up he noticed something gold in its stomach. The fish had eaten my ring!

you can't have your cake and eat it

you must choose between two things as it is impossible to have both at the same time

> A: My wife is the actress Sara Silk. She says she likes being famous but hates it when people stop her on the street to ask for an autograph. It's a big problem.
>
> B: Tell her *she can't have her cake and eat it*. If you're famous you must accept that people will recognise you.
>
> A: But the problem is they don't recognise her. People always mistake her for her rival Vicky Velvet!

A common way of using this proverb is the expression: *try to have your cake and eat it*. For example, *Oh, her! She always tries to have her cake and eat it.*

SIMILES AND METAPHORS

This section is a collection of some of the most useful and common similes and metaphors. Such expressions can be inventive and original but the most common ones are familiar enough to be clichés (see Foreign idioms section!) They are expressions which everyone understands instantly. They give information about behaviour, reactions, opinions and so on, without long explanations. Although similes and metaphors have the same purpose, they are expressed in different ways.

A simile is an expression which compares what you are talking about to an apparently unconnected object or situation. For example, *To Jenny, the bad news was like water off a duck's back* likens the effect of the bad news to the way water runs quickly off a duck's feathers. Water seems to have no effect on a duck—it soon shakes it off and looks dry again. In the same way the bad news has no effect on Jenny—it is soon shaken off and forgotten. All similes take the form **as . . . as . . .** or **like . . .**

A metaphor is a comparison which does not use **like** or **as**. For example, if you tell someone to *grasp the nettle*, you are comparing the activity of holding a plant which stings when touched, to what you wish them to do. In other words, the metaphor *grasp the nettle* describes doing something very unpleasant which takes courage!

as cool as a cucumber
as light as a feather
as regular as clockwork
as thick as two short planks
be unable to see the wood for the trees
get on like a house on fire
grasp the nettle
in a nutshell

like a red rag to a bull
like water off a duck's back
make a beeline for something
make a mountain out of a molehill
pour cold water on something
skeleton in the cupboard
storm in a teacup
taste of one's own medicine (a)

as cool as a cucumber

calm/not worried/in control

> A: Miss Wrinklie, the old age pensioner, was watching television when a man broke into her house.
>
> B: Poor woman, she must have been terrified.
>
> A: Actually, Miss Wrinklie was *as cool as a cucumber*. She hit the man over the head with her walking stick and immediately called the police!

as light as a feather

extremely light

> A: Have you moved that box yet?
>
> B: No, you told me it was as light as a feather but it's so heavy I can't lift it.
>
> A: It is *as light as a feather* — it's only the things inside which are heavy!

as regular as clockwork

very regular/habitual

> A: Mr Bolton comes to the bank every day to draw out £1000 in cash. He arrives at 10 o'clock *as regular as clockwork* but yesterday he didn't come at all.
>
> B: How strange. What had happened?
>
> A: He hadn't got any money left in his bank account!

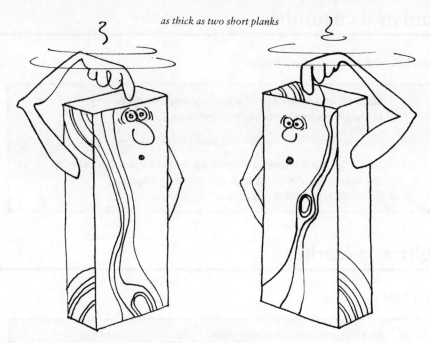

as thick as two (short) planks

very stupid/unintelligent

> A: I've been looking for my keys everywhere but I can't find them. Have you seen them?
>
> B: Honestly, you're *as thick as two short planks*! You're holding them in your hand!

This expression, which can also be shortened to **as thick as two planks**, makes a pun of **thick** which means **stupid** as well as the more normal meaning (ie the opposite of thin).

be unable to see the wood for the trees

be unable to see the important points of a situation due to concern over unimportant details

> A: It took me six months to solve the murder inquiry.
>
> B: Really? Why did it take so long, Inspector Kosh?
>
> A: There were so many confusing facts that for a long time I *couldn't see the wood for the trees*. However, my wife is now under arrest!

get on like a house on fire

enjoy the company of someone very much

> A: My father met my new boyfriend, Rodney, last week.
>
> B: Oh dear, I'm sure that didn't go very well. Your father doesn't like young men with red and green hair.
>
> A: Actually they *got on like a house on fire*. They discovered that they both like opera and talked about it all afternoon!

grasp the nettle

deal with a problem quickly and directly even though it may require some courage

> A: I borrowed Harry's best suit for a job interview. Unfortunately, afterwards I spilt black ink on it and now it's ruined.
>
> B: My advice is to *grasp the nettle* and tell Harry what's happened. The longer you don't tell him about it the more angry he'll be when he finds out.
>
> A: Yes, you're right—I must do it. But how do I tell him about the interview? It was for his job!

A **nettle** is a plant which grows wild and can sting if touched. The only way to avoid being hurt is to take hold of it quickly and **grasp** it firmly. Obviously this takes some courage!

grasp the nettle

in a nutshell

essentially/very concisely

> A: What's the matter with the plane?
>
> B: *In a nutshell*, the problem is that one wing has dropped off and both engines have stopped.
>
> A: Oh no! What shall we do, Captain?
>
> B: Well, you'd better tell the stewardess to cancel the film. There won't be time for it now!

in a nutshell

like a red rag to a bull

infuriating/causing great anger

> A: Last week I took a pair of new shoes back to the shoeshop because the heels had fallen off. I talked to the manager but he refused to give me my money back.
>
> B: That wasn't fair. How annoying.
>
> A: Yes I know. So when he said: 'Leave the shop or I'll call the police', it was *like a red rag to a bull* and I hit him over the head with my handbag!

Bulls are traditionally thought to be enraged by the colour red, which is why Spanish matadors use a cloak with a red lining for bullfights. However, the belief is a false one as bulls, like most animals, are colour-blind. When a bull approaches the matador it is attracted by the movement of the cloak and not by its colour.

like water off a duck's back

be unaffected by an unpleasant experience

> A: Anita Tutu, the ageing ballerina, is starring in a new production of 'Swan Lake'. All the newspaper critics said she was too old and should retire.
>
> B: Oh dear, I'm sure Miss Tutu was very upset when she read the reviews.
>
> A: No, the comments were *like water off a duck's back* to Anita. She invited all the critics to her house and told them she was still the best dancer in the world!

It's very common to shorten the saying by omitting **like**. For example, *It was water off a duck's back to Anita.*

make a beeline for something

go directly to something

> A: There's Gary Girth. He looks much thinner than when I last saw him.
>
> B: Yes, he's lost over thirty kilos by eating only carrots and lettuce for three months. He says he's going to lose another twenty kilos by Christmas.
>
> A: Then why is he *making a beeline for that enormous chocolate cake* covered in cream?

Bees spend the day flying from flower to flower to collect pollen. However, in the evening they return to their hives as quickly as possible and therefore fly in a straight line. They *make a beeline for home.*

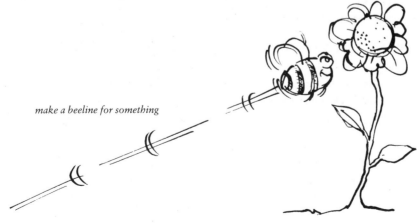

make a beeline for something

make a mountain out of a molehill

make a small problem seem very important/exaggerate a minor difficulty

> A: Doctor, I'm really frightened. I've just come back from Africa and I'm sure I've caught malaria. I sneezed twice this morning.
>
> B: Now Mr Worrier, you're *making a mountain out of a molehill*. All you have is a head cold!

A mole is a small wild animal which lives under the ground and digs tunnels through the soil. It leaves small heaps of soil on the surface of the ground and these are known as **molehills**.

make a mountain out of a molehill

pour cold water on something

make negative and unhelpful comments about something

> A: I talked to the bank manager today about opening a shop for the Eskimos in North Alaska.
>
> B: Did he *pour cold water on the idea*?
>
> A: Yes, he said it wasn't possible to lend me money for the venture because he didn't think Eskimos would be interested in buying fridges!

skeleton in the cupboard

an embarrassing secret from someone's past

> A: I feel very sure of being the next Prime Minister of England.
>
> B: Yes Mr Minor. But do you have any comments to make about the affair you had a year ago with Betty Buff, the film actress?
>
> A: Oh that. Well everyone has a *skeleton in the cupboard*. I don't know what all the fuss is about!

storm in a teacup

a small problem which is exaggerated

> A: This is disgraceful. I'm not paying the bill and I'm going to tell all my friends never to come to this restaurant again.
>
> B: Surely there's no need for that, sir—this is just a *storm in a teacup*.
>
> A: Not at all. Finding an old sock in my bowl of soup is a very serious matter!

storm in a teacup

a taste of one's own medicine

unpleasant action or words in return for an identical or similar experience

> A: I'm having a party. There'll be loud music playing until dawn. Would you like to come?
>
> B: I don't understand. You hate loud music.
>
> A: Yes you're right, but my neighbour keeps having noisy parties which wake me up so I've decided to give him *a taste of his own medicine*!

See: TURN THE TABLES which describes the reversal of good fortune with someone else.

a taste of one's own medicine

94

EXERCISES

Exercise A

Choose the right phrases to complete the following sentences.

1 Fred is so lazy he never leaves the house. He's a complete *couch cabbage/couch vegetable/couch potato*.

2 I'm sure that one day you'll be very rich but I'm not going to stick my *head out/ neck out/tongue out* and say exactly when it will happen.

3 Nicky is very intelligent and rather *blue stocking/grey stocking/blue sock*. She's happier reading a book about philosophy than dancing at a disco.

4 I've invited Simon on holiday with us but he's not interested in going abroad. I told him he was a *spare tyre/wet blanket/sour grape*.

5 Mrs Jest told me my car had been stolen. I was just about to phone the police when she told me it was a joke. She had just been *tearing me off a strip/ripping me off/winding me up*.

6 The old man wanted me to climb up onto the roof of his house to rescue his cat. I told him that was *easy come, easy go/easier said than done/easier done than said*.

7 So many things have gone wrong this week that when you cancelled our dinner date it was the *first straw/only straw/last straw*.

8 I thought I would be nervous, but when I made the speech I was *as cool as a cucumber/as cool as a marrow/as cool as a lettuce*.

9 Supermarkets are very good value, but you always *spend through the nose/pay through the nose/pay through the eyes* when you go to small shops.

10 I didn't have enough time to prepare the lecture so its rather *namby-pamby/ topsy-turvy/slapdash*.

Exercise B

Read this letter then fill in the expressions from the list below in the correct form.

ad nauseam
on tenterhooks
catch on the hop
headhunt
up to scratch
humdrum

look a gift horse in the mouth
high-flyer
a taste of one's own medicine
hurly-burly
chock-a-block
eat humble pie

The Park Hotel
London

Saturday, 19th August

Dear Lucia
    I arrived in London last Sunday. The city is _____1_____ with people but I enjoy the _____2_____ because it makes a change from my quiet little village in Switzerland.
    My friend, Tim, has invited me to dinner tonight. He works in advertising and is definitely a _____3_____. Apparently, he's the youngest director in the company and says that he's already been _____4_____ twice! Tim's very nice, but unfortunately he talks about his work _____5_____. I've tried giving him _____6_____ and telling him about my job but he just doesn't take the hint!
    I've made friends with an American woman called Alison who is staying in the room next to mine. She's quite a character! This morning she complained to the waiter that her breakfast wasn't _____7_____. The waiter looked furious, he stared at her for ages and I was _____8_____ wondering what was going to happen next. Then, without saying a word, he took the food back to the kitchen and brought her another breakfast.
    Tim is driving to Oxford tomorrow on business and asked me if I'd like a lift. I'm not someone who _____9_____ so I've accepted. I'll spend the day looking around all the old colleges - I've heard they're really beautiful.
    Anyway, I must stop now because I have to get ready for tonight - I'm going on a riverboat disco down the Thames. A taxi is going to collect me from my hotel in half an hour and I don't want to be _____10_____.
I'll write again soon.

       Lots of love
         Christine

Exercise C

Put the right expression into these extracts from magazines and newspapers (use only one expression in each extract).

1   **buzz word**   **status quo**   **junk mail**   **slapdash**

JUNKING _____

They call it direct marketing—we call it _____. You know those envelopes that thud on your doormat and promise their contents will change your life, if only you'll just open them and look inside? Well here's how you can have your revenge: save several of them and return them to the worst offender (the company that you receive most mailings from) in a large, heavy brown envelope.

Cosmopolitan

2   **clapped-out**   **macho**   **freebie**   **state-of-the-art**

LIBEL JUDGE SAYS SORRY FOR SLANDERING HIS '_____ VOLVO'

A judge made a public apology in court yesterday—to his car.

Colourful senior High Court judge Mr Justice Davies, 68, said he was sorry for calling his car a '_____ Volvo' during the Lord Linley libel action last week. 'I've apologised personally to it and promised it a good service,' he said.

Daily Mail

3   **from the sublime to the ridiculous**   **tit for tat**   **business as usual**
     as regular as clockwork

Unlike the ill-fated Clarissa, Saskia has a happy love life. She will marry her fiancé Sean Henderson, who works in the City, in July.

'We will still be filming so I will take a day off for the ceremony and then it is _____,' she said.

Mail on Sunday

4   **raconteur**   **underdog**   **toyboy**   **bimbo**

URSULA TO WED _____

Ageing screen goddess Ursula Andress is to wed an Italian _____ young enough to be her son. Ursula, 54, who was the first James Bond girl, has been living with baby-faced Fausto Fagone, 24, for four years.

News of the World

---

5   **burn yourself out**   **strike while the iron is hot**   **mind your Ps and Qs**
kowtow

GEMINI

This is a remarkable period of the year for career and professional interests— especially if you are involved in new creative schemes. However, you must _____ and not leave it to others to negotiate terms or finalise agreements.

Evening Standard

---

6   **raconteur**   **blarney**   **dosh**   **DIY**

HOW TRUE LOVE IS HAMMERED HOME

I must tell you about my husband after reading in your newspaper that women find men with _____ skills more attractive.

John had no _____ experience when we married. As I adore old properties, one wondered whether our marriage itself might need renovation.

But he has tackled every job, from plumbing to carpentry, plastering and bricklaying.

Mail on Sunday

---

7   **booze**   **rabbit**   **bumf**   **bonkers**

From _____, drugs, sex and scandal to happy families and clean living, Richard Dreyfuss is staging a rebirth. After 12 years apart, he's back with Spielberg as a guardian angel in 'Always', a tale of the heart and the hereafter.

Time Out

---

8   **ad nauseam**   **up to scratch**   **topsy-turvy**   **like water off a duck's back**

However, ideas, decor and atmosphere are nothing if the food does not come _____, so Simon recruited top chef David Wilby. With a CV that reads like something from the Good Food Guide, David believes it doesn't matter what you are cooking, the highest standards should be employed at all times.

In & Around The London Pavilion

---

9   **whinge**   **rabbit**   **hype**   **moonlight**

WE DON'T _____, WE'RE JUST UNLOVED, SAY TEACHERS

Teachers denied being '_____ing' wimps yesterday as they prepared to strike. Staff, who get 13 weeks holiday a year and an average salary of £14,000, say they are overworked, underpaid and unloved.

Evening Standard

---

10   **post mortems**   **sell-by dates**   **tête-à-têtes**   **sour grapes**

Confectioners may be tempted to consider changing their policy on _____, after a 91-year-old bar of Rowntree's chocolate proved perfectly edible.

The bar—which was sampled yesterday by Brigadier Malcolm Cubiss (retired), curator of a York military museum—was one of 1,000,000 sent by Queen Victoria at Christmas 1900 to British troops fighting the Boer War.

The Guardian

---

11   **moonlighting**   **squatting**   **headhunting**   **whingeing**

Julian Browne has been _____ from his job as features editor of the Sunday Times Magazine to write about cars for Southside since its third issue.

Southside

---

12   **as light as a feather**   **fuddy-duddy**   **as thick as two planks**
humdrum

Male models were voted 'drop-dead' gorgeous by 82% of women but were also reckoned _____. Rock stars were seen as the least intelligent and 52% rejected them as unreliable.

Daily Mail

Exercise D

Complete the following sentences with help from the pictures below.

1 You must make sure they agree to a _____ before you go ahead and accept the job.

2 I'm afraid I've got a _____. A long time ago I was arrested for drunk driving.

3 You are such a good cook—your cakes are always _____.

4 As soon as I saw you I knew we would _____ and become great friends.

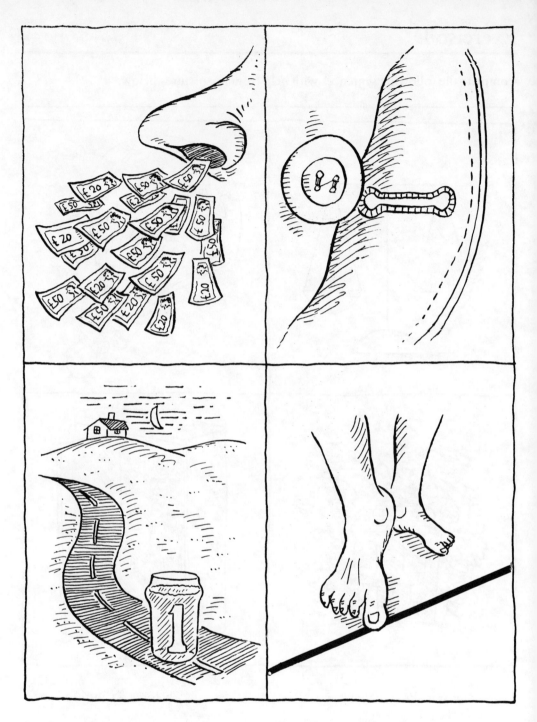

5 On my way out I was _____ by a man who wanted money.

6 I know it's late but I'm going to have _____ before I leave the pub.

7 Edward always does exactly as he wants; he never _____.

8 Harry loves the shop so much he doesn't mind _____ for the things they sell.

Exercise E

Choose the right phrases to complete the following sentences.

1 After my first marriage ended in divorce I decided never to marry again. I suppose it's a case of *once shy, twice bitten/once bitten, twice shy/once bitten, once shy.*

2 On the first day he started work I found out that he wasn't *per se/faux pas/au fait* with computers—in fact he couldn't even type.

3 I'm not sure if Lizzy will buy the house with me—she keeps *blowing hot and cold/changing hot and cold/blowing cold and hot* about it.

4 There was only one aeroplane on the tiny island and it turned out to be a *Keith Robinson/Heath Robinson/Hobson's choice* machine which looked as if it was held together with string!

5 Mr Saltzmann had only walked a few minutes from his house when he was *duffed up/bunged up/clapped-out* by a stranger who took all his money.

6 I don't want to disturb the *applecart/status quo/business as usual* so I'm not going to tell my boss that Linda is always late for work.

7 Every Friday at exactly 4.30 pm, Mr and Mrs White leave for the country. They're *as regular as a clock/as regular as clockwork/like a red rag to a bull.*

8 Phoebe is very intelligent and has always done well at school. That's why she has such a *blasé/forte/cliché* attitude to passing exams.

9 I know you think you'll get the job but *it's no use crying over spilt milk/one swallow doesn't make a summer/don't count your chickens before they hatch.* Wait until they have actually offered you the post before you celebrate.

10 The police said it was a *humdrum/topsy-turvy/tit for tat* crime. Apparently the two gangs are always fighting each other.

11 He deserves an extra special present, so I'm going to buy Simon a *state-of-the-art/flagship/squatter* television.

Exercise F

Put the right expression into these extracts from magazines and newspapers (use only one expression in each extract).

---

1 paparazzi   pooh-pooh   hurly-burly   claptrap

Councillor Julian Heather said, 'All the talk of improving public safety by better street lighting is proving to be just so much _____.'

The area's Neighbourhood Watch chairman Stephen Harwood said, 'I advise our members not to go down the alley at night.'

The Wandsworth Guardian

---

2 brouhaha   culture shock   gobbledegook   hype

Buzz words for one audience can be _____ for another. We have to explain in different, simpler terms the intent of the reforms for the man in the street and for the general body of staff.

The Guardian

---

3 business as usual   carte blanche   culture shock   hurly-burly

BUSH RUNNING AMERICA FROM HOSPITAL BED

Eager to present a picture of _____, officials emphasised that tests showed that Mr Bush, aged 66, had not suffered a heart attack or any permanent heart damage and he was running the nation from his hospital suite.

The Times

---

4 claptrap   dosh   faux pas   hype

HOW TO MASTER _____

It doesn't matter who you know, or how much talent you possess, all you have to do is become a master of _____.

Use the media in the right way and your profile will be as high as you wish. Andrew Croft sets out in detail the tricks of the trade in his new book '_____: the Essential Guide to Marketing Yourself'.

Today

---

5 **ghetto blasters**   **old bangers**   **white elephants**   **bonkers**

Through 4000 miles of desert and sun, 208 _____ have just completed an epic road race that Australia has taken to its heart.

7 Days

---

6 **flagship**   **state-of-the-art**   **hype**   **high-flyer**

ITN'S _____ SAILS ON WITHOUT SIR ALASTAIR

Sir Alastair Burnet, aged 62, whose retirement from his job at Independent Television news was announced yesterday, will not be replaced as senior newscaster.

The existing news team of Trevor McDonald, Julia Somerville and Alastair Stewart, backed by Fiona Armstrong, will continue to present the _____ programme.

The Times

---

7 **macho**   **white elephant**   **faux pas**   **bête noire**

HOW TO WIN ON SPORTS DAY

As the school sports day gets into full swing, not all parents realise that their own performance beside (and on) the sports track can make or break their children's reputations with classmates and teachers.

A pale blue Rolls Royce is the biggest _____, according to Charlotte Lewis. 'I've watched boys say "How could he?" when their fathers have driven up in extremely smart cars.'

The Times

---

8 **barking up the wrong tree**   **looking a gift horse in the mouth**
upsetting the applecart   **blowing hot and cold**

Executives who own a pet dog are _____. The cat is the designer pet of the Nineties. Researchers, who have spent 15 years matching pets to social types, predict that soon the animal you choose will say as much about you as your car.

Today

---

9 **forte**   **status quo**   **flavour of the month**   **sell-by date**

He is just a nasty, bigoted old man whose _____ is long past. He should leave public life as soon as possible.

The Guardian

---

10 **yuppie**   **buff**   **toyboy**   **riff-raff**

Costya Vasilchishin is a Soviet _____. He has no car phone; indeed he has no car. But at 25 he earns five times the average salary for his work on the new Russian bourse (stock exchange), and he looks well on the way to having a heart attack by 40.

The Independent

---

11 **yuppies**   **toyboys**   **paparazzi**   **blue stockings**

Princess Diana and Sun royal photographer, Arthur Edwards, have enjoyed a special relationship ever since he rushed to her aid in 1980.

Di, then Lady Diana Spencer, was being pursued by the worlds' _____ trying to get candid photographs of the girl who was to be Prince Charles' bride.

The Sun

---

12 **plonk**   **gunge**   **one for the road**   **junk food**

Free trade, friendship and cheap wine. It seemed like a good idea at the time. We were joining a Common Market where produce was plentiful and prices were low.

After a hard day we would all sit down together for a glass of _____ and a song.

The Sun

Exercise G

Read this diary then fill in the gaps with the appropriate expressions from the list below.

bonkers

run the gauntlet

whodunnit

raconteur

ding-dong

easy come, easy go

let the cat out of the bag

sour grapes

eat humble pie

cliffhanger

SUNDAY
This afternoon I watched a film on TV. It was a ___1___ from the 1950s. Even though it was made such a long time ago it was very good. It was supposed to be a real ___2___ but unfortunately my brother ___3___ and told me who the murderer was.

MONDAY
Today I was interviewed by a journalist about my work. I had to ___4___ of all sorts of difficult questions — I was glad when it was over. He said that our rivals thought our company was making low quality products. I told him it was just ___5___ because we were so successful.

TUESDAY
The head of the Union, Mr Bolt, came to see me this afternoon. He told me that the workers in the factory would strike unless they received more money. I said he was ___6___; there had been a pay rise only a month ago. The discussion turned into a ___7___ and he walked out in a temper.

WEDNESDAY
I met an old friend for lunch. Alec is a real ___8___ and he told me some fabulous stories about his travels abroad. Apparently he won £5,000 at a casino in the south of France and then someone stole it from his hotel room the same night! I said I would have been furious but Alec just smiled and replied, '___9___.'

THURSDAY
There was a vote in the factory to see how many workers wanted to strike. The result was that the majority wanted to continue working for the same money. So when Mr Bolt came to see me again he had to ___10___ and apologise for getting angry earlier in the week.

Exercise H

Complete the following sentences with help from the pictures below.

1 The explanation the accountant gave me was very complicated but
_____ he told me I've spent too much money!

2 Everyone has to _____ sometime, but no one wants to be there when
it happens!

3 I know _____, but I refuse to believe the stories in the newspapers.
I'm sure my father has never broken the law.

4 We'll pay you £100 000 if you tell us the name of the politician. Honestly, it's
_____.

5   You don't take me seriously. Whenever I make a suggestion, you always
    _____ on it.

6   They are both so involved in the problem that they can't _____.

7   Danny hasn't stopped talking about his holiday all evening. I wish he'd
    _____.

8   Miss Jones used to tell me what to do all day but now I'm the boss the
    _____.

Exercise I

Put the right expression into these extracts from magazines and newspapers (use only one expression in each extract).

---

1   **carte blanche**   **short shrift**   **Hobson's choice**   **white elephant**

In the past 20 years the hotel has become renowned for protecting its famous guests from unwanted publicity. Anyone who courts the cameras, on the premises or even on the street outside is given _____ by the owners. It upsets the other guests and is bad for business.

Sunday Times Magazine

---

2   **blarney**   **buzzwords**   **hotchpotch**   **claptrap**

Unable to face the prospect of one city emerging a clear loser, the talk was of a decision that could mature with time. Yesterday's _____ were *Zeitschienenmodell (time rail model)* . . . and *Rutschbahnbremse (the split function compromise with slide brake)*.

The Independent

---

3   **blow hot and cold**   **grasp the nettle**   **let sleeping dogs lie**   **make a beeline**

I feel it is time to _____ and openly acknowledge, as members of the Dutch medical profession have done, that euthanasia is, in a few specified situations, not just morally defensible but a necessary act of humanity.

Observer Magazine

---

4   **flogging**   **headhunting**   **pooh-poohing**   **hyping**

John had saved about £1000. To raise more, he took on a market stall and found he enjoyed _____ ladies' dresses. From here, he made a modest move to a suburban men's clothes shop in Edgware, north London, soon followed by a second branch in Golders Green.

News of the World Magazine

5 **corny**   **user-friendly**   **Hobson's choice**   **flavour of the month**

Then he took on the lease of the shop in South Molton Street. It was a good move. John hired a publicity agent and was introduced to the right people. In August 1976, 'Ebony' opened for business.

'I became _____,' John recalls. He and his wife, Ruth, moved from a one-bedroomed flat in Primrose Hill to a £500,000 luxury home.

News of the World Magazine

---

6 **bimbo**   **macho**   **user-friendly**   **nightmare scenario**

IT'S STILL A MAN'S WORLD AT THE OFFICE

Women suffer unfair discrimination at work because most companies are run on the basis of a masculine culture, it was claimed today.

The _____ approach measures commitment on the basis of hours spent at the workplace and not how men use that time or how good they are at their jobs.

Evening Standard

---

7 **torn off a strip**   **flogged**   **ripped off**   **bunged up**

I know that by now all my goods will have been _____, but I continue to hope that there may be some clue left behind that will lead the police to the burglars. I want to feel safe again.

Evening Standard

---

8 **highflyer**   **yuppie**   **headhunter**   **golden parachute**

ARE _____S REALLY NECESSARY?

Both Malcolm Crump and Neil Anthony independently calculated that if they were putting six or more jobs to _____s a year then someone on the permanent staff would more than pay for him or herself.

A _____ charges roughly one third of the salary attached to the appointment. Thus, if one is talking about a £60,000 job there is a simple equation: 6 × £20,000 fee = £120,000.

Human Resources Magazine

111

9 **culture shock**   **carte blanche**   **moonlight**   **freebie**

FOUR DAYS OF DRINKS ON THE EMPTY HOUSE

Every drinker's dream came true for a group of friends who walked into a pub to find the landlord absent.

Gallons of beer, 100 bottles of spirits, wines and soft drinks were drunk and stocks of crisps, nuts and snacks vanished as the party went on for four days.

One of the partygoers said: 'It was great while it lasted. People just don't miss a golden opportunity like that to have a _____.'

Evening Standard

---

10 **nightmare scenario**   **brouhaha**   **blarney**   **blitz**

THAMES TELEVISION

7.30 CORONATION STREET

Jim MacDonald's plan to build an extension in the back yard already seems to contain all the ingredients for a major _____. It looks as if the main thrust of opposition will come from Vera Duckworth.

Evening Standard

---

11 **bimbo**   **humdrum**   **headhunt**   **kowtow**

YOUNG LOVE AND ORDINARY MURDER

It was a _____ murder of an ordinary girl, and that is its real interest. The events that preceded it were ordinary. The love story was not extraordinary. On the contrary it was a student love affair in all its embarrassing, confused, experimental and passionate normality.

The Independent

Exercise J

Complete the expressions in each of the following sentences.

1 Helen explained her problem but the policeman *gave her short* _____. He didn't want to help at all and told her not to bother him.

2 An old school friend that I hadn't seen for years telephoned me to ask me out to dinner. I *gave him the cold* _____ because I didn't want to see him again.

3 I would love to see the world but I hate travelling in planes—they're my _____ *noire*.

4 Angela is the best architect in the country, so we gave her _____ *blanche* to design whatever she wanted.

5 Don't write a letter to complain; just forget about it. It's best to *let sleeping* _____ *lie*.

6 We thought that buying this land would be a good investment but it's been a complete *white* _____.

7 It's not that I want to *keep up with the* _____, it's just that it's time we bought a new car.

8 David says it's _____ *choice*. We can't pay so we will have to leave the country forever.

9 I'd obviously *caught her on the* _____. She hadn't even packed her suitcase.

10 When Leo *kicks the* _____, he wants everyone to have a big party to celebrate.

Exercise K

Fill the gaps in this letter of complaint with the appropriate expressions from the list below.

---

slapdash
as thick as two short planks
gunge
gobbledegook
whingeing

pièce de resistance
stolen his thunder
buff
bunged up
hyped

106 Charlton Road,
Kidderminster,
Worcestershire.

Friday 27th February

The Manager
Theatre Royal
Hamchester

Dear Sir
 Yesterday evening I attended a performance of 'Sherlock Holmes Gives Up'. It was _____1_____ as the _____2_____ of the season, but I have to disagree. The whole evening was a disaster from start to finish, I have never seen such a _____3_____ production.
 To begin with, the curtain went up over half an hour late and a member of your staff made an announcement. He said that because Sir Nigel Carmichael was ill, Sherlock Holmes would be played by Betty Barnacle.
 I am not a theatre _____4_____ but I do know that actors should at least be able to remember their lines. Mr Holmes read his from a book and at one point Dr Watson had to help him find the correct page! The lady who played the housekeeper had a bad cold and was so _____5_____ that her words sounded like _____6_____. The so-called plot was complete rubbish. In all the stories about Sherlock Holmes, he always finds the answer to the mystery, but in the second act of the play he tells Watson that the murder is too difficult to solve. Sherlock Holmes is supposed to be the best detective in the world not _____7_____! The whole audience was disappointed. Several people got up and left.
 In Act Three Watson solves the entire mystery himself and names the murderer. Holmes, the 'great' detective, then spends the rest of the play _____8_____ and complaining that Watson has _____9_____.
 When the curtain finally came down, I thought the worst was over. However, on leaving my seat I found that I had been sitting on some grey _____10_____ - possibly chewing gum.
 I enclose the dry-cleaning bill and the two tickets for the show. I expect a cheque by return of post.

Yours faithfully
Mrs Angela Fotherington

114

Exercise L

Complete the following sentences with help from the pictures below.

1 I always try to learn from my mistakes because _____.

2 I would love to wear a bikini this summer but I must get rid of my _____ first.

3 I was pleased when Joe got _____ and was told to tidy his office. Usually he tells other people what to do.

4 When I suggested we should go to a disco it was like a _____. He didn't speak to me for days.

5 My grandfather _____ on about his garden all the time. Yesterday he talked for two hours about it!

6 It seemed important at the time but now I realise it was just a _____. I can't even remember what the argument was about!

7 Alicia says she doesn't like working hard but she wants to earn lots of money. I told her she was trying to _____.

8 As soon as we arrived at the hotel, I _____ for the pool because I love swimming.

ANSWER KEY

Exercise A

1   couch potato
2   neck out
3   blue stocking
4   wet blanket
5   winding me up
6   easier said than done
7   last straw
8   as cool as a cucumber
9   pay through the nose
10 slapdash

Exercise B

1   chock-a-block
2   hurly-burly
3   high-flyer
4   headhunted
5   ad nauseam
6   a taste of his own medicine
7   up to scratch
8   on tenterhooks
9   looks a gift horse in the mouth
10 caught on the hop

Exercise C

1   junk mail
2   clapped-out
3   business as usual
4   toyboy
5   strike while the iron is hot
6   DIY
7   booze
8   up to scratch
9   whinge
10 sell-by dates
11 moonlighting
12 as thick as two planks

Exercise D

1   golden parachute
2   skeleton in the cupboard
3   as light as a feather
4   get on like a house on fire
5   buttonholed
6   one for the road
7   toes the line
8   paying through the nose

Exercise E

1   once bitten, twice shy
2   au fait
3   blowing hot and cold
4   Heath Robinson
5   duffed up
6   status quo
7   as regular as clockwork
8   blasé
9   don't count your chickens before
    they hatch
10 tit for tat
11 state-of-the-art

Exercise F

1   claptrap
2   gobbledegook
3   business as usual
4   hype
5   old bangers
6   flagship
7   faux pas
8   barking up the wrong tree
9   sell-by date
10 yuppie
11 paparazzi
12 plonk

Exercise G

1. whodunnit
2. cliffhanger
3. let the cat out of the bag
4. run the gauntlet
5. sour grapes
6. bonkers
7. ding-dong
8. raconteur
9. Easy come, easy go
10. eat humble pie

Exercise H

1. in a nutshell
2. kick the bucket
3. there's no smoke without fire
4. money for old rope
5. pour cold water
6. see the wood for the trees
7. put a sock in it
8. tables are turned

Exercise I

1. short shrift
2. buzzwords
3. grasp the nettle
4. flogging
5. flavour of the month
6. macho
7. flogged
8. headhunter
9. freebie
10. brouhaha
11. humdrum

Exercise J

1. shrift
2. shoulder
3. bête
4. carte
5. dogs
6. elephant
7. Joneses
8. Hobson's
9. hop
10. bucket

Exercise K

1. hyped
2. pièce de resistance
3. slapdash
4. buff
5. bunged up
6. gobbledegook
7. as thick as two short planks
8. whingeing
9. stolen his thunder
10. gunge

Exercise L

1. it's no use crying over spilt milk
2. spare tyre
3. a taste of his own medicine
4. red rag to a bull
5. rabbits
6. storm in a teacup
7. have her cake and eat it
8. made a beeline

INDEX